Classic
BRITISH BIKES

Classic
BRITISH BIKES

Mac McDiarmid

PARRAGON

Page 1: Rickman Interceptor; the final flowering of Royal Enfield's mighty 736cc parallel twin. Page 2: 1937 Triumph Speed Twin; the machine which launched over 30 years of British motorcycle superiority. Page 3: 1938 Velocette KSS was the classic British sports single of its era. Page 5: A 1934 Matchless Model X4 side-valve V-twin.

This is a Parragon Book

© Parragon 1997
Reprinted in 1998

Parragon Publishing
13 Whiteladies Road
Clifton
Bristol BS8 1PB

Designed, produced and packaged by
Stonecastle Graphics Ltd.,
Old Chapel Studio, Plain Road, Marden,
Tonbridge, Kent TN12 9LS, United Kingdom

Edited by Philip de Ste. Croix

ISBN 0-75252-224-8

Printed in Italy

Photographic credits:
All photographs by **Mac McDiarmid** except:

Andrew Morland: pages 2, 3, 11 (top), 17,
21 (below), 26, 30, 36 (below), 37 (below), 41, 44,
48 (below), 50, 58, 65, 79 (top).

EMAP (Classic Bike/Classic Motorcycle):
pages 5, 14, 15 (top), 32, 33 (left), 33 (right), 35,
36 (top), 38, 51 (below), 52 (top), 52 (below), 54,
63 (below), 64 (top), 64 (below), 68 (below), 71
(left), 71 (right).

Figures and data in this book are quoted in
Imperial measurements first, with the metric
equivalents noted in brackets.

Contents

Introduction

THE FIRST working internal combustion engine was built just over 120 years ago by Nikolaus August Otto, who gave his name – 'Otto cycle' – to the four-stroke principles on which it operated. When Gottlieb Daimler installed a derivative of this primitive machine into a wood-framed 'motor cycle' in 1885 he can have had little idea what he was starting (his first 'motor car' came two years later). In 1894 two more Germans, Heinrich Hildebrand and Alois Wolfmüller, created the first powered two-wheeler to be put into commercial production. There were even plans to

build them under licence in Britain. As tried and tested as manned missions to Jupiter are now, the venture flopped and the duo soon went broke.

By 1897 the Paris-based Werner brothers were making motorcycles with the engine above the front wheel, later opening a second factory in London. The first British engine, the Beeston, dates from this period. For a time France and Belgium led the world in engine technology with companies such as de Dion and Minerva, but by the early 1900s British pioneers such as Holden, Humber, Raleigh and the Coventry Motor Company had joined the fray.

The first motorcycles were nothing more than motorized bicycles, and it was natural that existing makers of the latter should turn to the former. The capital of British push-bike production was Coventry and, to a lesser extent, the West Midlands as a whole. Almost overnight these fumbling beginnings transformed the region into the epicentre of the motorcycle world.

The roll-call of British motorcycle manufacturers which emerged is truly staggering. As well as those pioneering enterprises with chapters expressly devoted to them, it is possible to name, with some effort of memory: AJW, Ambassador, Armstrong, Ascot-Pullin, BAT, Beardmore Precision, Beeston, Blackburne, Bradbury, Calthorpe, Campion, CCM (still going), Chater-Lea, Clyno, Cotton, Coventry-Eagle, Coventry-Victor, Diamond, DMW, DOT, Dunelt, EMC, Gamage, Grindlay-Peerless, Hazlewood, Henley, Hobart, Holden, Humber, JAP (they briefly built complete bikes), Juno, Lagonda, Lea-Francis, Levis, LGC, Lily, McEvoy, Majestic, Mars, Martinsyde, Matador, Mohawk, Monarch, Montgomery, Morris, Ner-a-Car, New Gerrard, New Hudson, New Scale, NLG, Norman, NUT, Premier, Quadrant, Quasar, QUB, Raleigh, Silk, Simplex, Sprite, Stevens, Sun, Tandon, Vindec, Wassell, Weslake, Wilkinson, Williamson, Wooler, Zenith and Zephyr.

If that leaves you breathless, then consider this: I now turn to a reference book and find L&C, Lancer, Leonard, Lethbridge, Little Giant, Lincoln-

Left: In the early years, many manufacturers relied on outside engine suppliers. This 1913 BAT No2 Light Roadster uses a 770cc JAP side-valve V-twin.

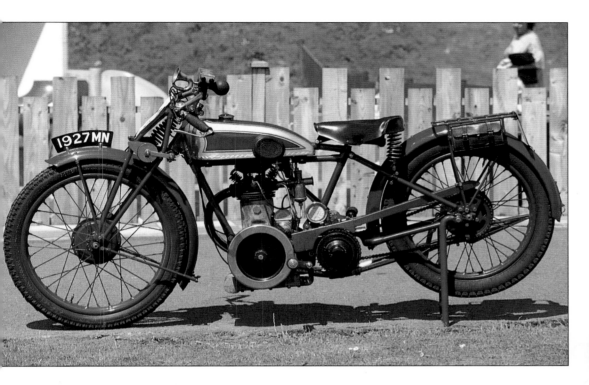

roots lay in a mind-set that believed singles and twins (initially vee, later parallel) were more than sufficient, and that, anyway, any alternative must be too costly to produce. There was actually no shortage of exotic prototypes. It was simply that they never saw the light of day. The relative failure of such high-profile exceptions as there were – Ariel's Square Four, Sunbeam's S7, for instance – can only have persuaded conservatives that they were right.

But the purpose of this book is less to condemn than to celebrate decades of success.

Left: Although mainly associated with two-strokes, DOT ('Devoid of Trouble') also produced potent four-strokes, such as this oil-cooled, Bradshaw-engined, ohv single.
Below: 1928 598cc Beardmore Precision side-valve Model C.

Elk, Lloyd, London . . . and more. And that's merely part of the 'Ls'. A great many people threw all their money, effort and imagination into creating the two-wheeled heritage we now enjoy. Most, it's probably true, contributed more enthusiasm than skill. But who can blame them, for what exciting times those 'can-do' early days must have been?

And many others had the talent and foresight to create what became the greatest motorcycle industry in the world. In taking on and ultimately taming these new-fangled, two-wheeled contraptions, they showed vision, flair – and, probably most of all, persistence. They put British technology – most

of all empirical West Midlands know-how – firmly on the map. To them we can be grateful for a shining legacy.

Equally, mention must be made of the decay and collapse of this once-great edifice. All empires appear to develop a sense of complacency that leads to their ultimate decline, and the British motorcycle industry was no exception. If the early era was daring often to the point of recklessness, the later, more monolithic years were characterized by short-term profit-seeking at the expense of investment; and by a lack of board-room imagination that became almost institutionalized. But in part the

Dawn of Technology

O NE THING may already have struck you about the famous marques featuring elsewhere in this volume: with very few exceptions, the machines they produced were vertical singles or twins. This conformity did not arrive by accident, and there was more to it than the fact that singles, in particular, are simple to produce. It arose because motorcycles – including their engines – need to be relatively light, compact and slim.

In the early days this last factor, at least, encouraged straight fours at the luxury end of the

market. Unlike modern across-the-frame multis, these were arranged fore-and-aft. The formula offered great flexibility at the expense of an unwieldy machine. Its chief proponents were American companies such as Henderson, the Belgian FN, the German Windhoff 'Vierzylinder', and (most enduringly), the Danish Nimbus.

But there were British fours too. Best-known was the Austin-engined Brough, but the world's first was the 385cc Binks, briefly produced in transverse as well as longitudinal layout. Until 1916, Wilkinson,

Above: Girder-type forks (these belong to a DOT) dominated the scene from the earliest years until the Fifties. Left: Early fours were almost exclusively longitudinal, such as this 648cc Wilkinson TMC.

now more famous for razors, produced TAC and TMC fours, both air- and liquid-cooled, of 676 and later 848cc. The TAC – Touring Auto Cycle – was piloted by means of a steering wheel. Other notable exceptions were the V-four Matchless Silver Hawk, flat twins from James, Humber, Blackburne and Douglas, threes from Redrup (radial) Humber and Scott (parallel) and, of course, Ariel's Square Four.

But in the earliest days, even debate about engine configuration was premature, for it was yet to be agreed where the best location for the engine might be. All manner of positions were championed until what we now think of as the most natural – the 'Werner position', so-called after the brothers of that name – became accepted. At the opposite extreme, the French Dufaux had a seven-cylinder radial engine in the rear wheel, while 20 years later the German Megola housed its radial five in the front one.

Yet novelty there was, for in 1900 almost everything now considered essential to motorcycling had yet to be invented. Rex produced the first telescopic forks as early as 1906, and BAT the first sprung frame at about the same time. JAP created the first overhead-valve V-twins as early as 1906 (they also built a 660cc three for Dennell), the same year P&M offered two-speed transmission, including a clutch. Internally-expanding brakes and 'single-sided' wheel mounting were seen on James machines in 1908.

Alfred Scott came up with all manner of firsts, including kick starts, 'monoshock' rear ends, efficient radiators and rotary inlet valves. In 1912, Rudge created the first belt-type multi-speeder (20 of them) in the Multi, although Matchless created the first true multi-speeders shortly later. The Twenties were widely regarded as motorcycling's golden age, when four-valve heads first appeared and overhead cams (Peugot had introduced double overhead cams in 1913) became almost commonplace. Disc brakes appeared on Douglas motorcycles in the early Twenties, a decade that also saw hydraulic brakes on the technically advanced, monocoque-framed Ascot Pullin. Almost everything since has been refinement.

Right: V-twins were popular for their compactness, ease of manufacture and, in the days before multi-speed transmissions, strong pulling power.

9

AJS

ALBERT JOHN Stevens – 'AJS' – had the right background to become a principal founder of the British motorcycle industry. The son of a blacksmith, 'Jack' was one of five brothers, raised in the Black Country hotbed of light engineering. He built his first internal combustion engine as early as 1897, although it was to be after the turn of century that he supplied the first commercial powerplant. These went initially to other manufacturers such as the Wearwell Motor Carriage Co. They were simple devices of about 125cc, mounted high on a sloping front downtube, below the steering head.

In 1909, AJ Stevens & Co was founded to manufacture complete motorcycles, with premises in Retreat Street, Wolverhampton. The first true AJS machines appeared in 1911, a 292cc side-valve two-speeder. One was entered in the Isle of Man TT races that year, AJS's first major competition outing.

By 1914 AJS had made their mark on motorcycling. In that year derivatives of the 1911 machine, now enlarged to a full 350cc and boasting a novel 'two-by-two' four-speed chain drive, contested the Junior TT. The result was sensational: first, second, third, fourth and sixth places. This in turn led to a surge in orders, and a move to bigger premises. Although the First World War prevented an immediate TT defence, in 1920 AJS again won the Junior TT, repeating the feat in the following two years. These post-war machines were advanced overhead-valve models, later christened 'Big Port' engines, with hemispherical combustion chambers, aluminium pistons and three-speeds. One 350 also gave away 150cc to win the 500cc Senior TT in 1921.

Ajay prospered on these successes, producing a range of side-valve singles in 350 and 500cc, plus an 800cc V-twin. 1927 brought their first overhead camshaft design, chain-driven, not unlike the later, legendary 7R racer. Although this was not as successful as new 'cammy' racers from Norton and Velocette, a special 250cc version won the 1930 Lightweight TT ridden by the legendary Jimmy Guthrie (it would be 1954 before they would win a TT again).

1931 brought the most ambitious new model so far. The S3 tourer was a 496cc transverse V-twin (not unlike a modern Moto Guzzi), with alloy cylinder heads and many advanced features and a clever ergonomic design. It cost a great deal to develop but was not a sales success. Having also diversified into cars, commercial vehicles and even radios, the development of the S3 exposed the

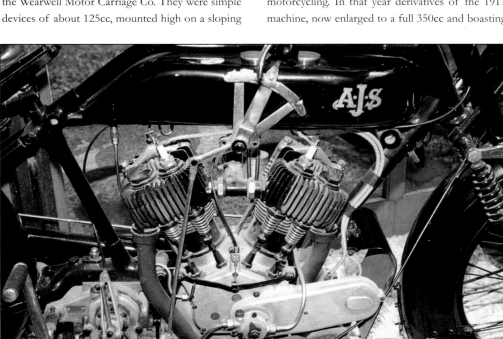

Left: Although chiefly associated with singles, in the Twenties AJS produced machines such as this 800cc V-twin. A later V-twin, the S3, was transverse.

10

company's lack of a solid financial base. Then, just as it seemed that AJS would disappear, the Matchless company of Plumstead, London stepped in to save the name. Production at once transferred from Wolverhampton. In 1938 the company was again reconstituted, as Associated Motor Cycles (AMC), for a time also combining the Sunbeam marque.

Although AJS roadster models thereafter were predominantly re-badged Matchlesses, the AJS name continued to be associated with technically advanced racing projects: notably the V-four, Porcupine and 350cc 7R, which in turn begat the

Below: This 1928 K4 350cc side-valve single was a popular sports roadster, although by this time Ajay's first overhead camshaft machines had appeared.

11

Above: The imposing Colonial 1000, built in 1938, the same year AJS was swallowed into the giant Associated Motor Cycles empire.

500cc Matchless G50, still the dominant force in classic racing today. Ironically (for a company which won the first TT), Matchless were initially opposed to competition, and it was only the persuasive efforts of die-hard racers such as George Rowley which caused them to relent. This led first to success at Brooklands, later in trials (through the ohc 350cc Trophy models), and ultimately to a succession of ambitious Ajay racers. AMC finally went broke in 1967, although some 'AJS' two-stroke scramblers and the 745cc Norton-engined Model 33 (Matchless G15) were later built by Andover Norton.

500cc V-FOUR

The 500cc V-four was one of the most audacious motorcycles in British history, although its successes were few. Although originally launched as a roadster at the 1935 London motorcycle show, the Bert Collier-designed 495cc AJS mercifully never found its way onto public roads. With four cylinders arranged in a 60 degree Vee, chain-driven single overhead camshafts in each pair of cylinders and a further chain driving a front-mounted supercharger,

when first raced in 1936 it was air-cooled, slow, unreliable and only just about rideable. By 1939 it was liquid-cooled, more reliable, and more than a match for the supercharged Gilera fours. But it handled like a pig.

1936 had seen the bike fail badly at the Isle of Man TT, due to rear-cylinder overheating. No development work was done on the engine in 1937, partly because engineer Matt Wright didn't want the thing in his race shop: 'It frightened me just to look

SPECIFICATION	AJS V-FOUR RACER
ENGINE	liquid-cooled 495cc ohc V-four
POWER	55bhp
TRANSMISSION	4-speed
FUEL TANK	N/A
WEIGHT	N/A
TOP SPEED	130mph (209km/h)

Below: Magnificent, but a real handful: the racing V-four.

at it.' For the 1938 TT, however, he dispensed with the supercharger, installing four carburettors instead. The bike retired yet again. A year later it earned two hard-won but disappointing finishes at the Isle of Man TT: Walter Rusk placed 11th, Bob Foster 13th.

At the Ulster GP, however, the 500 was able to exploit its 55bhp and 130mph (209km/h) potential. In sprinting away from Serafini's Gilera, Rusk became the first man ever to record a lap speed of 100mph (161km/h), although the machine later retired with a broken fork link. But the Ajay's violent, weaving progress up the seven-mile (11km) Clady Straight went immediately into Irish folk-lore.

The Second World War effectively ended the V4's development. Although the bike was raced post-war – in 1946 Jock West won on it at Chimay – supercharging was outlawed by the time the world championship began in 1949. And the AJS was simply too heavy to be competitive in normally aspirated form.

AJS PORCUPINE

Like the V-four, the Porcupine – so-called because of its spiky cylinder finning – was another ambitious AJS project thwarted by the ban on supercharging. The parallel twin featured gear-driven twin-overhead cams, but AJS never fully redesigned it to suit normal induction, and power was a disappointing 40bhp. Later E93 versions, with inclined cylinders, made around 55bhp at 7600rpm, still substantially less than the Gilera four. After seven years AJS returned to their roots with the sort of pedigree lightweight single on which their name had been founded: the 7R.

Above and right: The striking 'Porcupine' 500cc dohc parallel twin was another ambitious AJS racer handicapped by the post-war ban on supercharging.

SPECIFICATION	AJS PORCUPINE
ENGINE	air-cooled 498cc dohc parallel twin
POWER	up to 55bhp @ 7600rpm
TRANSMISSION	4-speed
FUEL TANK	N/A
WEIGHT	N/A
TOP SPEED	140mph (225km/h)

AJS 7R

A descendant of the ohc racing R7 singles of the Thirties, the 350cc 7R which appeared in 1948 was everything the Porcupine was not: light, agile, with good handling and power enough in the right hands. Nicknamed the 'Boy's Racer', it featured an easy-to-maintain chain-driven overhead camshaft and scored countless wins in National-level competition. Its finest achievement came in 1952 when the great Bob McIntyre took one not only to victory in the Junior Manx GP, but to second place in the Senior, as well. In the mid-Fifties a triple cam, three-valve version was developed by Jack Williams. Production lasted until 1962, although a 500cc derivative, the Matchless G50, continued.

POST-WAR ROADSTERS

In the post-war era there was little difference between models badged 'AJS' and those labelled 'Matchless', all being built and designed in the same Plumstead facility (see page 38). Most notable were the twins, beginning with the Model 20 (Matchless G9) of 1948, itself AMC's interpretation of Edward Turner's seminal Triumph Speed Twin. Featuring an alloy head, light alloy con-rods (like Norton's twin), a three-bearing crankshaft to minimise flex, and a non-unit four-speed gearbox, the 380lb (172kg)

Below: The cam drive housing of this 1952 7R can clearly be seen on the right side of the cylinder barrel. This arrangement was far easier to produce and maintain than the Manx Norton's bevel drive. The later Matchless G50 looked substantially the same.

Above: Probably the hottest-ever AJS roadster, this 1960 110mph (177km/h) Model 31CSR Sports Twin was similar to Matchless' G12 CSR.

machine initially produced 26bhp, good for around 85mph (137km/h). However, like all AMC twins, it gained a reputation for excessive vibration.

The AJS 30 CSR (Matchless G11CSR) was a tuned version of the 1956-on 592cc parallel twin, itself a development of the earlier 498cc twin. Tuning work lay in the capable hands of Jack Williams, later to become famous for his work on the 7R and G50 racers. Higher compression, hotter camshaft, better port shapes and exhaust boosted power from 34 to almost 40bhp at 6000rpm, for a genuine 100mph-plus.

Right: AJS were also active off-road, producing machines such as this 1956 16MS competition, a 347cc ohv four-speed single.

When the Model 30 was bored out from 72.8 to 79.3mm to become 646cc, the hottest Ajay, the Model 31 CSR (Matchless G12 CSR) was born. Producing 46bhp at 6500rpm, it scaled 430lb (195kg) and could reach 110mph (177km/h). Such a device won the prestigious Thruxton 500-miler in 1960. Some CSRs were sold as Monarch and Apache machines in the USA.

Ariel

LIKE MANY of its contemporaries, the Ariel company began life manufacturing bicycles, achieving an important if unspectacular breakthrough when in 1870 its leading lights, James Starley and William Hillman, invented the tensioned wire-spoked wheel. Although bolting an engine into one of these flimsy devices seemed the natural step as the internal combustion revolution gathered pace, in 1898 the firm's first powered vehicle was a de Dion-engined quadricycle, a sort of four-wheeled bicycle. (In the early days the company also manufactured sewing machines.) It was not until around 1902 and takeover by the Sangster family's company, Components Ltd., that they began to get serious about two-wheelers. The Sangsters – initially Charles, later Jack – were to become key figures in the British motorcycle industry, and were already engaged in the manufacture of cars. The first model built at their Selly Oak, Birmingham factory, used a Kerry engine, later replaced by 4hp White and Poppe side-valve units. Ariel later built similar engines under licence.

Charles Sangster himself was no mean engineer, having designed a sophisticated three-

Above and left: Ariel's response to the parallel twin race was the Val Page-designed KH500 Hunter Twin, introduced in 1948. The example left dates from 1953, the one above from one year later.

speed two-stroke with clutch and kick start which might have succeeded had the world war not intervened. Ariel's first 20 years were otherwise marked by a succession of largely unremarkable machines, notably side-valvers singles and V-twins of 498 and 669cc respectively, and an inlet-over-exhaust 998cc V-twin.

During the early Twenties the Ariel range extended from a 586cc Blackburne-engined single to a 992cc MAG-engined V-twin, but it was at this time that young Jack Sangster demonstrated a talent quite different – but even more far-reaching – than that of his father. Sangster junior was simply a remarkable judge of talent who, in a few short years, enlisted three of the great British designers to the Ariel cause: chief designer Val Page, Bert Hopwood and, in 1927, Edward Turner himself.

Turner's most enduring contribution to Ariel was the immortal Square Four. He had created the basic 497cc overhead cam design in a small machine shop in Dulwich, South London, hawking it around several manufacturers until Jack Sangster saw its value. The resulting prototype, housed in the same frame as a 500cc 'sloper' single, was the sensation of the Olympia motor cycle show. The year was just 1930.

Although the four was not a huge commercial success, with the departure of Page in 1932, Turner set about revitalizing the Ariel range (a task he was later to repeat with Triumph), most successfully with the Red Hunter range of 500cc and later 350 and 250cc singles.

After the Second World War, with Ariel now part of the giant BSA Group and Page again in charge of design, what was effectively Ariel's final generation of models took shape. Predictably these were led by ohv parallel twins. The first of these, the 500cc KH, was solid but uninspired, did not sell well and was withdrawn in 1957. Thereafter Ariel's big twin pretensions lay with the 650cc Huntmaster series introduced in 1954, essentially a re-jigged BSA A10. If Ariel retained a separate identity, it was most clearly seen in the world of trials, where the exploits of Ulsterman Sammy Miller on his 500cc single (registration GOV132) became legendary.

Page's other main four-stroke contribution were the last, 'four pipe', versions of the Square Four. But it was his two-strokes which for many

were the most memorable. Introduced in 1958 the Leader and Arrow range of 250cc twins was a valiant and reasonably successful attempt to lead strokers away from their cheap, utilitarian image. Effectively this was the company's last throw of the dice, for Ariel was increasingly subsumed into the amorphous BSA after the closure of Selly Oak in 1960.

ARIEL SQUARE FOUR

One of the most imposing British motorcycles ever produced, Turner's enduring four was essentially two vertical twins on a common crankcase, comprised paired transverse crankshafts, geared together at their centres. A single chain-driven overhead camshaft controlled the valves and the wet-sump crankcases split horizontally. In its original 498cc form this was an astonishingly light

SPECIFICATION	ARIEL SQUARE FOUR MKII
ENGINE	air-cooled 996cc ohv square four
POWER	42bhp @ 5800rpm
TRANSMISSION	4-speed
FUEL TANK	5 gallons (22.7 litres)
WEIGHT (dry)	485lb (220kg)
TOP SPEED	103mph (166km/h)

(330lb, 150kg) and compact powerplant, but in growing to 596 and ultimately 996cc, it changed character completely.

Below: Although Edward Turner's original ohc Square Four was conceived as a solo sports machine, this push-rod 1000cc MkII is ideally suited to sidecar lugging. Note telescopic forks and plunger rear suspension.

much heavier flywheels. The 4G produced 38bhp at 5500rpm. In 1939, plunger rear suspension was added. After the war the 600cc version disappeared, and by 1948 the 1000 had telescopic forks and was some 33lb (15kg) lighter, largely thanks to a light alloy cylinder head and block.

1954 brought the final Square Four, Page's MkII 'four-piper'. Power had risen to 42bhp, but plunger rear suspension was retained in an age when swinging forks were becoming commonplace on machines of this price. The last Ariel Squariel rolled off the Selly Oak production line in 1958, although a much revised development, the Healey 1000, was produced in Redditch in limited numbers in the mid-Seventies.

Left and below: Girder forks and rigid rear end mark this Square Four 1000cc 4G as a pre-1939 example (actually 1937). A 600cc stablemate, the 4F, failed to survive the Second World War.

Throughout its life, however, the 'Squariel' had one major weakness. The cylinder head was prone to distortion, as the rear cylinders sat in the heat shadow of the front ones, and early attempts to race the four, albeit in supercharged form, were plagued by problems of heads warping. Although a normally-aspirated version managed to take the coveted Maudes Trophy by covering 700 miles (1127km) in 668 minutes, overheating and the inefficient 'cruciform' inlet tract would always impose a limit on the Squariel's performance.

In 1937 a revised range of fours appeared. Available in both 599 (the 4F) and 996cc (4G) form, these featured push-rod valve actuation, vertically-split crankcases and, partly to suit sidecar use, very

SPECIFICATION	ARIEL LEADER (GOLDEN ARROW)
ENGINE	air-cooled 249cc two-stroke twin
POWER	16bhp @ 6400rpm (20bhp @ 6650rpm)
TRANSMISSION	4-speed
FUEL TANK	2.5 gallons (11.4 litres) (3 gallons/13.6 litres)
WEIGHT (dry)	330lb (150kg) (305lb/138kg)
TOP SPEED	68mph (109km/h) (78mph/126km/h)

ARIEL LEADER AND ARROW

With its pressed-steel beam frame and unit-construction, twin-cylinder, two-stroke engine, Val Page's Ariel 1958 Leader was unlike any motorcycle seen before. Fairly light and agile, with lively performance, it was clean, functional – and radical. The engine, inspired by the German Adler twin, was smooth and responsive, although petroil lubrication remained a necessary chore. As well as a generous standard specification, an extensive range of options was available.

In 1959 the Leader was joined by a sports version, the Arrow, more conventional looking, but still with the same frame (in which fuel was carried under the seat in the manner of Honda's much later Gold Wing). Later a 'super sports' Golden Arrow appeared, along with a 197cc version. Racing derivatives achieved moderate success.

Right: The Arrow was one of the most innovative post-war British designs, combining a 250cc two-stroke twin with a novel steel 'monocoque' chassis.

19

Brough

YOUNG GEORGE Brough could scarcely have had an upbringing better designed to propel him into the new age of motorcycling. As early as the 1890s, his father, William, had built his own car, barely a decade after the invention of this new contraption. A tricycle and later a two-wheeler followed, all with proprietary de Dion engines, as Brough senior established himself as a pioneer of the new revolution.

In 1906, at the age of 16, young George Brough had competed in his first John O'Groats to Land's End trial on one of his father's machines. By all accounts this was a troubled and miserable experience which can only have served to persuade him to create something better. He later went into partnership with his father William building Brough machines, but it was a less than happy partnership, as his energy and new ideas were often unwelcome.

Inevitably, in 1919 George set up in business on his own in premises in Nottingham which would remain his company's base until 1935. (Brough senior continued producing motorcycles, initially with 496cc ABC engines, later with flat twin Brough engines of up to 810cc.) From the outset George had a clear philosophy. His motorcycles would utilize the very best components and technology then available, selling for high prices to discerning customers only. They would in every way be superior to those available elsewhere, including from his father: they would be Brough Superiors. The first was shown at the Olympia motorcycle show of 1920, and first independently tested in 1921.

Below: Typical of the breed, this 1934 Brough Superior 11-50 combined the very best of available components to give earth-shattering performance for its time.

SPECIFICATION	BROUGH SUPERIOR SS100
ENGINE	air-cooled 990cc ohv V-twin
POWER	50bhp
TRANSMISSION	4-speed
FUEL TANK	4.25 gallons (19.3 litres)
WEIGHT	426lb (193kg)
TOP SPEED	100mph (161km/h)

Soon dubbed the 'Rolls-Royce of motorcycles', this machine set the mould for most of George's subsequent models. Whilst most British machines of the time had single cylinder engines, this was powered by a 986cc ohv JAP engine, driving through a three-speed Sturmey Archer gearbox. There were high quality Brampton forks, and other equipment such as lighting, normally sold at extra cost, came with the standard price of £175. The tester lavished praise on the performance (80mph, 129km/h), handling and overall quality of the machine.

Bread-and-butter Brough Superiors – if there was such a thing – used V-twin engines, mainly from JAP but also from MAG and, latterly, Matchless. But George was equally renowned for more startling designs, such as a 796cc straight four based on an Austin 7 car engine (1932). There were also prototype V-fours and straight fours and a striking transverse four, the 1939 'Dream', a sort of early Honda Gold Wing. Brough Superiors were also commonly engaged in record-breaking and racing –

Right: Perhaps the best-known Brough of all, T.E. Lawrence's (Lawrence of Arabia) SS100. In 1932 its 998cc offered a genuine 100mph (161km/h).

most memorably at Brooklands, where Noel Pope's 124mph (200km/h) lap record can never be beaten. In a straight line, Broughs set world records in 1929 (128.75mph, 207.2km/h) and 1937 (169.68mph, 273.07km/h).

But the most prized conventional Broughs were the SS models. The SS100 featured an ohv engine, whilst the SS80 was a 998cc side-valve. The SS100 – the 100 signified mph around Brooklands – evolved over almost 20 years, latterly with a superbly refined 990cc Matchless engine. Although often billed as 'the world's fastest motorcycle' in standard form, even this gave best to the awesome SS100 Pendine model, guaranteed to exceed 110mph (177km/h).

As well as for sheer excellence, there is one other reason George's creations are so prized. In almost 20 years of motorcycle production, perhaps as few as 3000 Brough Superiors were built, one

Above: The heart of almost every Brough was a big V-twin.

reason why they easily fetch £30,000 when appearing for sale today. Although the Second World War effectively ended production, such is the power of the legend that a small company in Kent has recently been attempting to produce replicas of these very superior machines.

21

BSA

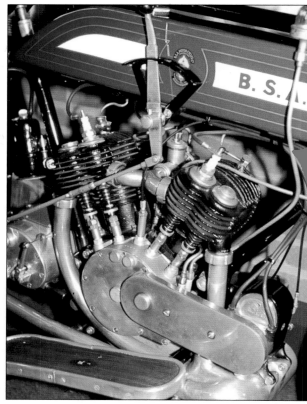

FOR MANY years BSA was the giant of the British motorcycle industry and for a time also the biggest motorcycle manufacturer on earth. The company began life in 1862 as Birmingham Small Arms, an association of 14 gunsmiths formed to supply arms for British forces in the Crimean War. Even today, three stacked rifles remains the company's famous logo.

A year after its foundation, BSA moved into the Small Heath factory which was to be its home for the next 110 years. In the 1880s it began making bicycles, and came up with its first powered two-wheeler in 1903. This diversification has always been a BSA hallmark. During the Second World War, when they produced 126,000 military M20 motorcycles, the group comprised no less than 67 factories engaged in a huge array of industrial activities.

Even during the First World War, BSA was a huge industrial complex. Initially famed for single cylinder models such as the Model H and model K, in 1919 it introduced the first of a notable series of

If sidecar-hauling big V-twins (above) typified BSA's early years, the humble 125cc Bantam (left) was an even bigger post-war success.

V-twins. Although, like Triumph, the company was never particularly competition-minded, the Thirties marked the debut of a model which was ultimately to lead to the immortal Gold Star. This began life in 1931 as Herbert Perkins' Blue Star, evolved into the Empire Star and then, via Wal Handley's exploits at

Brooklands, into Val Page's 1938 Gold Star. Post-war versions were substantially different, but the Goldie range is arguably the classic single of all UK designs.

By the mid-Fifties BSA had acquired Triumph, Sunbeam and many other marques and were the largest motorcycle company in the world – although their best-selling model, the Bantam, was essentially a pre-war German DKW RT125 design. Although BSA's bread-and-butter was straightforward commuter machines, the post-war years brought a succession of highly successful parallel twins, beginning with the A7 Shooting Star.

In 1960 the company reported profits in excess of £9 million, and BSA's horizons seemed to know no bounds. Yet the following decade saw the company slow to respond to the influx of technically advanced, cheap new motorcycles from Japan. Ironically, during this period BSA boasted a highly sophisticated development department at 'space age' Umberslade Hall, and perhaps the most automated motorcycle production line outside Japan. Yet for all this potential, the company flapped around like a headless chicken, producing a succession of failures in search of a replacement for the venerable Bantam. These included the Dandy and Beagle commuter bikes, a 250cc scooter and the catastrophic Ariel-3 tricycle. By the early Seventies, the group's losses were almost as great as their profits had been a decade before. Although the Rocket-3/Triumph Trident offered a glimmer of hope (see page 70), the effort of attempting to compete with the Japanese, notably with the BSA Fury/Triumph Bandit, eventually crippled them. By 1972 they were broke.

Manganese Bronze, by then the owners of Norton, acquired the BSA Group, mainly for its remaining profitable divisions (car bodies, sintered products etc). A proposed motorcycle rescue plan was thwarted by a workers' sit-in at Meriden, from which emerged the government-backed Triumph Cooperative. After the BSA collapse, Norton Villiers Triumph (NVT) took over remaining motorcycle operations, now at Shenstone, whilst both BSA's Small Heath factory and Norton's Wolverhampton plant were closed. From this

Above: The General Post Office's ubiquitous runabout, this 1961 Bantam, like all the rest, derives from a pre-war DKW design. Both the first Yamaha and Harley-Davidson two-strokes evolved from the same German RT125 machine.

emerged Norton Motors (the rotary project), which passed through a succession of owners before ending up by default in the hands of the Canadian Aquilini family (along with the UK rights to the BSA motorcycle name).

Two other parts of the original NVT stake, BSA Co. and Andover Norton, were later disposed of in management buy-outs. Bill Colquhuon's BSA Co. produced Rotax-engined military bikes, plus Yamaha-based 'Bushman' machines for Third World markets. Mike Jackson's Andover Norton turned out Commando spares as well as importing AP Lockheed and other products. In 1991 the two merged to become a new BSA Group. This was in turn taken over by a Southampton-based group to become BSA Regal in 1994. The group has diverse light engineering interests, and last year unveiled a new BSA model, the Gold SR. This harnesses a Yamaha SR400 engine in an unashamedly Gold Star-styled chassis. Ironically, Japan is by far the biggest customer for this born-again Goldie.

BSA GOLD STAR

The one and only DBD34 'Goldie' was both the ultimate clubman's production racer and the single-cylinder street racer of the Fifties. BSA's best-loved name came from the coveted Brooklands gold star, awarded for 100mph (161km/h) laps at the legendary banked Surrey circuit (where, ironically, Yamaha's UK base is now located). In 1937 Wal Handley (as in Handley's Bends on the Isle of Man) had lapped Brooklands at 107.57mph (173.11km/h) on a tuned Empire Star BSA. A year later M24 'replicas' were the first to bear the Gold Star name.

Post-war Goldies, apart from being some of the most antisocial motorcycles ever produced, were in fact little more than hopped-up ohv B31/32 and B33/34 roadsters. The 350 appeared in 1947,

The original pre-war 'Gold Star' (such as the 1938 example pictured left) was based upon the Model M24. The star itself – but not the tank badge (above) was awarded for 100mph (161km/h) laps at the banked Brooklands circuit near Weybridge.

the B34 500 in September 1949. The 500's first success was off-road, winning 11 gold medals at the 1949 International Six Days Trial. In 1950 it acquired swing-arm rear suspension, and in a few short years had achieved such utter domination of the Clubman's TT that the viability of the races themselves were threatened. The Goldie was becoming too fast for its own good. Of 37 Junior entries in 1955, for instance, no less than 33 were Gold Stars.

Although produced in many specifications, the ultimate DBD34 Goldie had a huge Amal GP

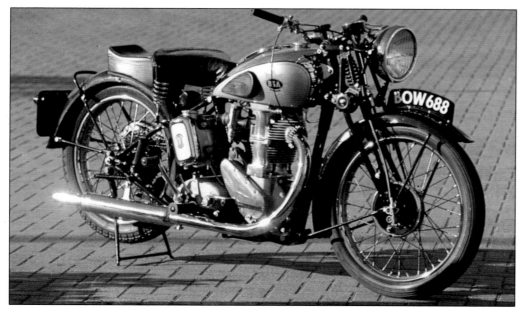

carb, no tickover, no air-cleaner, almost no silencing and fouled plugs like a two-stroke. In road trim it produced around 38bhp at 7000rpm, perhaps 5bhp more in race trim, allowing it to sweep the board at numerous Clubman's Manx GPs.

SPECIFICATION	DBD34 GOLD STAR
ENGINE	air-cooled 499cc ohv single
POWER	38bhp @ 7000rpm
TRANSMISSION	4-speed
FUEL TANK	4.0 gallons (18.2 litres)
WEIGHT (dry)	420lb (191kg)
TOP SPEED	110mph (177km/h)

Above and right: Post-war 'Goldies' were little more than reworked B31 and B33 roadsters — but the reworking was undeniably sublime. As well as becoming the most desirable single on the street, the Gold Star swept all before it in the Isle of Man's Clubmans TT. Even roadsters could comfortably exceed 100mph (161km/h).

Gold Star production ceased in 1962 when BSA declared their highly-strung hooligan single uneconomic to produce. Instead they set about developing a modest 250cc single, the C15, for trials and scrambles. This grew by degrees to 250, 440 and 500cc, gave Jeff Smith two world motocross titles, and transforming off-road sport.

POST-WAR TWINS

BSA's first post-war big twin, the 500cc Model A7, first came under public gaze at the Paris Motorcycle Show of 1946. Public reaction was favourable, but the bike's wasn't: performance proved to be disappointing, with a tendency to 'run-on' through self-ignition.

Cue Bert Hopwood, one of the most creative spirits in post-war British motorcycle design and the man also responsible for Norton's enduring Dominator. Hopwood redesigned the 500cc BSA twin into the 650cc A10 Golden Flash. This in turn generated a better A7, plus a sports 500 known as the Star Twin.

In 1952 the Star Twin made one of the most impressive attempts on the Maudes Trophy, awarded for feats of exceptional motorcycle endurance. Three Star Twins were ridden 1000 miles (1609km) to the ISDT in Austria, competed with distinction, then continued until each machine had completed 4900 miles (7885km). Not surprisingly, this earned BSA the coveted trophy, and the twin a reputation for mechanical strength.

The unit-construction BSA A50/A65 series followed early in 1962, prompted by Triumph's similar move. As well as eliminating the primary chain adjustment, the new twins had better electrics, weighed some 30lb (13.6kg) less than their predecessors, and were significantly less expensive than their Triumph competitors. They had clean,

SPECIFICATION	BSA SPITFIRE
ENGINE	air-cooled 654cc ohv vertical twin
POWER	up to 56bhp @ 7250rpm
TRANSMISSION	4-speed
FUEL TANK	4.0 gallons (18.2 litres)
WEIGHT (dry)	423lb (192kg)
TOP SPEED	110mph (177km/h)

Above: This lovely 1960 A10 Super Rocket shows the clean lines and unfussy details for which the 650cc twin was particularly renowned.

neat lines – perhaps too neat, because many considered the styling bland. But the first A65 claimed only 38bhp, and there was soon some concern about main bearing and oil pump failures. For whatever reason, the public wasn't impressed.

The performance datum during the early Sixties was of course Triumph's T120 Bonneville, whilst Norton set the yardstick for handling. BSA twins, on the other hand, were ideal sidecar hacks with a reputation for robustness rather than sparkling looks or performance.

True, BSA had created some worthy contenders, notably the A10RGS Rocket Gold Star twin. But these were specialized machines produced in relatively small numbers. It wasn't until the arrival of the Spitfire in 1965 that BSA truly entered the sports twin fray. A development of the twin-carb A65L Lightning, this was a much more single-minded beast. With vibrant red paintwork, alloy wheel rims, close-ratio gears, high-compression pistons and substantially less weight, this was the Beezer they'd been waiting for.

Left: By the time this 500cc A7 was produced in 1961, early teething troubles had been overcome.

The first Spitfire, with racing-style Amal GP carburettors and hot camshafts, claimed a potent 55bhp. Later examples were slightly de-tuned, if less raucous, with Concentric carbs and slightly less compression. The chassis, on the other hand, was only slightly different from 'cooking' BSA twins. And, worst of all, the short-stroke twin vibrated savagely at high revs.

1968 brought the last of the Spitfires, the MkIV, with a twin leading shoe front brake and audacious 150mph (241km) speedometer. Although a revised range of twins with oil-bearing frames appeared in 1970, these were unattractively styled and increasingly dated in overall design.

Above: One of the 500cc A7 Star Twins which made such an impact on the Maudes trophy in 1952.

Douglas

WHILST MOST major British motorcycle manufacturers followed a largely conventional and similar approach, Douglas was one which resolutely set its own style. In this respect, and even more in the choice of engine layout, the Kingswood, Bristol company has often been compared with BMW, who also specialized in horizontally-opposed twin-cylinder machines for the classier end of the market. The very first Douglas machine, and the last, was of this design.

The Douglas company began motorcycle production in 1907, using a 350cc engine originally designed by JJ Barter. Barter's Light Motors company had previously built an unusual single-cylinder machine, later doubled up into the flat twin for the 200cc 'Fairy' model. Although these were unsuccessful, Barter interested the Douglas foundry into taking up the design and after a slow start the project took off.

Despite their rather staid later associations,

Douglas soon gained their first competition success. In 1910, within three years of producing their first motorcycle in 1907, they took the coveted team prize in the International Six Days Trial. Two years later, WH Bashall brought them their first TT win, the 1912 Junior. Such triumphs paved the way to making the company a major manufacturer during the First World War, supplying the army with some 70,000 machines.

Further successes followed: the first 500cc machine to lap Brooklands at 100mph (161km/h) in 1921; Senior TT victory in 1923; Sidecar TT laurels the same year (with a strange banking outfit). 'Duggies' had become so established that even King George V acquired one. Whatever else they might offer, 'the best twins' always exuded an aura of class. On the other hand they produced a bewildering array of models, never seeming to devote long enough to each to get it truly right. No less varied were their other interests: Douglas also built aero and stationary engines, Vespa scooters, trucks and even dabbled with cars.

The company's best models were probably the EW series in the Twenties, and the outstanding but rare Endeavour of the Thirties. But regrettably, Douglas became as well-known for financial crises as for their treasured flat twins, and had already been taken over by BAC in 1935. Military business was brisk during the Second World War (including 20,000 generators alone), but the post-war years hit

Left: This 1911 example clearly shows the horizontally opposed twin cylinders forever associated with Douglas machines. Later models, however, favoured a transverse engine layout.

28

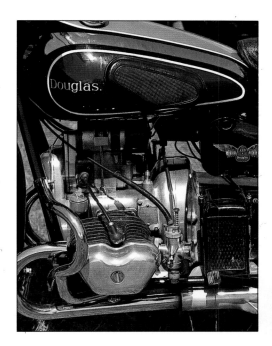

the company severely. In 1948 the receiver was called in, forcing the company to 'rationalize' with a line of models all based on same 350cc twin as the T35. At the time, the decision seemed sound. The 1949 'Sports' model was capable of 84mph (135km/h), and dubbed 'the world's fastest 350 roadster'. But by the time the Dragonfly succeeded the 'Mark' series in 1954, things were very different.

The Dragonfly was in many ways an advanced and novel design, with excellent cooling through its horizontally opposed cylinders and a car-type single plate clutch (although the final drive was by chain), Earles-type Reynolds front forks and swing-arm rear suspension. Handling and steering were light yet precise, it toured well, and the brakes were good for the time. But the roadsters were heavy and expensive for their size and even the rev-happy racers were soon eclipsed by BSA's all-conquering Gold Star. A promising 500cc prototype was shown in 1951, but never went into production. Additionally, Douglas' new owners, Westinghouse, seemed more interested in the production of Vespa scooters than the regeneration of the motorcycle range, and by the time motorcycle production ceased in 1957, only 1570 Dragonflies had been built. What was left of the company, Douglas (Sales and Service) Ltd., continued to import and assemble Vespa scooters and later Gilera motorcycles.

Although exceptionally refined and well-built, post-war Douglas twins such as this 1949 Mk3 (above) and 1957 Dragonfly (right) were increasingly left behind in the horsepower race, mainly in the face of larger capacity rivals. The latter was one of the very last machines to leave the factory.

SPECIFICATION	Douglas Dragonfly
ENGINE	air-cooled ohv 348cc flat twin
POWER	17bhp @ 5500rpm
TRANSMISSION	4-speed
WEIGHT	380lb (172kg)
FUEL TANK	3.5 gallons (15.9 litres)
TOP SPEED	72mph (116km/h)

Excelsior

'EXCELSIOR' WAS certainly a popular name during motorcycling's formative years, with two German and one American company sharing the name. But the most enduring of the four began life in 1896 as Bayliss, Thomas and Co., building bicycles in – where else? – Coventry. They were possibly the first British manufacturer of powered two-wheelers, initially using motors from Minerva, Werner and de Dion.

After the First World War, production moved to Tyseley, Birmingham when control passed to the Walker family, who built up a broad range of models from 98 to 1000cc. Most of the engines employed at this time were bought in from Villiers, Blackburne and JAP, plus a monstrous Condor-engined single of 850cc. Road-racing was ever high on the agenda, most notably with JAP-engined machines of 173 and 248cc. The factory's first major success came with Leslie Crabtree's victory in the 1929 Lightweight TT. A road-going 'replica', the B14, was quickly created for an eager public, becoming Excelsior's premier model.

Like New Imperial, Excelsior had the misfortune to reach their heyday in the depths of depression. In 1931 the factory almost captured the world speed record when their 'Silver Comet' supercharged 1000cc JAP-engined V-twin clocked 163mph (262km/h) but was unable to complete the return run. At the opposite capacity extreme, 1933 brought Ike Hatch's legendary Blackburne-engined 'Mechanical Marvel', a 250cc twin-carb, twin-cam, pushrod, radial four-valve design of sensational complexity on which Syd Gleave again won on the Island.

Below: The overhead camshaft 250cc Excelsior Manxman such as this 1936 model, produced around 15bhp.

SPECIFICATION	EXCELSIOR MANXMAN 250 (ROADSTER)
ENGINE	air-cooled 246cc ohc single
POWER	15bhp
TRANSMISSION	4-speed
FUEL TANK	3 gallons (13.6 litres)
WEIGHT (dry)	297lb (135kg)
TOP SPEED	75mph (121km/h)

This time, however, the Marvel's complexity ensured that there would be no replicas, for the company immediately set about creating a new range of overhead cam models. The Manxman series ultimately comprised 248, 348 and 498cc models, some also with four-valve heads. Blackburne's Ike Hatch was again the designer. Both road and competition models were sold, the latter becoming a formidable clubman's racer. The 250, in particular, continued to prosper in competition after the war.

The company as a whole did less well. Having approached the Second World War with the 1937 98cc Villiers-engined Autobyke, a forerunner of the commuter moped (they also built a 98cc two-stroke Sprite for Corgi), they continued in similarly humble manner when peace returned. The 98cc Consort, for instance, employed a mere two speeds and little by way of suspension. But the Talisman, unveiled in 1949, was a two-stroke of a different order. With a 243cc two-stroke twin engine, this was a precursor of many machines which were to follow. With its 180 degree crank, it was remarkably smooth, also benefiting from proper suspension at both ends (although a true swing-arm rear end would not

SPECIFICATION	EXCELSIOR TALISMAN
ENGINE	air-cooled 244cc two-stroke parallel twin
POWER	12bhp @ 4000rpm
TRANSMISSION	4-speed
FUEL TANK	3.5 gallons (15.9 litres)
WEIGHT (dry)	250lb (113kg)
TOP SPEED	65mph (105km/h)

The Talisman twin (above) used the marque's first in-house engine, a far cry from the very earliest Excelsior, this 1902 machine (below) with a De Dion-engine built by Bayliss and Thomas.

arrive until 1953). Regrettably, despite steady updating, twin-carb sports and a later 328cc version, sales were poor. In the early Sixties the 148cc Monarch, an attempt to cash in on the scooter boom, was no more successful and Excelsior folded in 1965.

31

Francis-Barnett

'FANNY B' never made any exotic machines, but for almost half a century kept Britain supplied with indispensable bread and butter two-wheelers. Although chiefly associated with two-stroke singles, the Coventry factory began life in 1919 with side-valve JAPs of 293 and 346cc, and for much of the pre-war era numbered similar machines amongst their range.

In the Thirties, there was also the Stag, a neat 248cc Blackburne-powered vehicle; and the 250 Cruiser, a scooterish device which made a better stab than most at appealing to the non-enthusiast market.

Two-strokes had arrived in 1924, supplied by the ubiquitous Villiers in capacities from 147 to 344cc – the latter a twin. The same year brought the introduction of their unique bolted-together frames which, although they sound flimsy, were fully triangulated and deceptively stiff: 'built like a bridge' was the slogan.

After the war, the range became entirely two-stroke, still with Villiers engines, now ranging from 98 to 248cc. In 1947 the company joined James in the AMC empire, and a decade later abandoned the Villiers connection in favour of in-house two-strokes designed by Vincente Piatti (later responsible for Suzuki's TSCC cylinder head technology). Partly due to poor assembly, the venture was not a success and Fanny B looked yet again to the Villiers power which had not only served it well on the road, but given considerable success in trails and scrambles. By this time, however, FBs were indistinguishable from James, and the the two sank together in 1964.

Below: One of the more radical Fanny B's, a 1959 Cruiser, with full rear enclosure but familiar two-stroke power.

Greeves

GREEVES WAS another manufacturer which pinned its flag to the Villiers banner, but this time with a distinctly sporting bent. Bert Greeves was already an elderly man when he created his first motorcycle in 1951, although he was no stranger to mechanical contrivances. As well as working for Heenan and Froude, famous for their dynos, he was an original thinker who seemed scarcely to let a week pass without creating some contraption or other.

In 1951 this was a prototype competition machine powered by a three-speed Villiers two-stroke single. The frame was a neat steel duplex, but it was the suspension (rooted in the design of Greeve's 'Invacar' invalid carriage) that grabbed the attention. Rubber bushes provided the springing and damping at both ends, offering an unheard-of six (152mm) and four inches (102mm) of travel at front and rear respectively. Production models arrived in September 1953, a 197cc four-speeder, shortly followed by a 242cc version powered by a British Anzani engine.

Whilst roadster such as the 250 Sportsman

Right: A 250c racer being hustled around Silverstone – the circuit which gave it its name – in 1965.

sold only modestly, Greeves machines enjoyed considerable success at trials, road-racing and, most of all, scrambles. Undoubtedly their finest hour came with Dave Bickers' 1960 European championship. That success led to the Hawkstone model, the road-racing equivalent of which emerged as the Silverstone, using a Villiers Mk34A engine with a Greeves top-end. From 1964 Greeves built their own Challenger engines, one of the first of which brought Gordon Keith victory in the 1964 Manx Grand Prix. Greeves effectively expired in 1977 with the retirement of its founder.

Left: Bert Greeves' novel front suspension can clearly be seen in this shot of a 344cc Oulton model. Both wheels were sprung by self-damping rubber bushes, a system which sounds crude but offered a superb ride.

Hesketh

THE HOUSE of Lords and Formula One car racing are an odd route to motorcycle production, but that is precisely the course taken by Lord Alexander Hesketh. A renowned patriot, the noble lord somehow took it into his head to create a flagship British motorcycle of the highest quality and specification. Sadly, it didn't work out.

But it was impressive, at least to look at. A V-twin engine layout was chosen, influenced by the then-revered Ducati and Moto Guzzi vees, but with a nod to British tradition in the form of Vincent. Yet, whilst Phil Vincent had been a radical, the Hesketh V1000 was in most respects profoundly conventional. It had four valves per cylinder and twin camshafts; true the first British roadster so equipped, but these were already commonplace in Japanese and a few Italian machines.

The Daventry-built motorcycle was, however, impressively specified – largely with Japanese and German components – hand-finished, visually imposing, heavy – and hugely expensive at £4995. The frame was similar to Colin Seeley's Ducati design, but was executed in Renolds 531 tube and much lighter. The first production models arrived

Above: The 992cc V-twin engine boasted two camshafts and four valves per cylinder, producing 85bhp. Only around 179 examples were built.

Below: Possibly one of the most aristocratic of motorcycles and certainly hugely imposing, the V1000 was a valiant attempt to create a true British 'superbike'.

six months late in 1983 after prototypes were slated by the press – the gear-change, in particular, was appalling. The noble venture lasted only briefly, with just 139 bikes built. A later attempt at resurrection fostered another 40 machines and was even less long-lived.

SPECIFICATION	HESKETH V1000
ENGINE	air-cooled 992cc dohc V-twin
POWER	85bhp @ 6500rpm
TRANSMISSION	5-speed
FUEL TANK	5 gallons (22.7 litres)
WEIGHT (dry)	506lb (230kg)
TOP SPEED	136mph (219km/h)

HRD

HOWARD RAYMOND Davies' brief but glorious adventure could scarcely have enjoyed a better start. His company was only months old when he raced to victory in the 1925 Senior TT on one of his own machines. Two years later the great Freddie Dixon added the Junior TT to HRD's list of successes.

A former First World War airman, Davies was second on a Sunbeam in the 1914 TT at the tender age of 19. In the 1921 Senior – on a 350 – he went one better for AJS, for whom he was racing manager. From then on, bad luck dogged his racing and in 1924 he resolved to ride a machine he could depend on – his own. HRD motorcycles was

formed. The first 'factory' was a house in Wolverhampton.

With EJ Massey, he created three models: the race-tuned, JAP-engined 500cc 90; the 344cc ohv 80; and the 500cc side-valve 70/S. Component specifications were high and the machines were of very racy appearance. When Bert le Vack added to the TT win with a host of 500cc Brooklands

Below: The JAP-engined 500cc ohv Super 90 was the cream of HRD's brief career.

records, HRD became established as desirable machines. In 1926 a new duplex frame appeared, a new 600cc model 90 and, for customers who could not afford the very best from these 'Leaders in Design and Speed', a pair of 'cooking' models, the 350cc HD65 or 500cc HD75.

It seems, however, that sport was far dearer than commerce to the heart of Mr HRD, for his company went bankrupt shortly after the 1928 motorcycle show. The name and rights passed briefly to OK-Supreme, only to be sold on again to another great innovator: Phil Vincent.

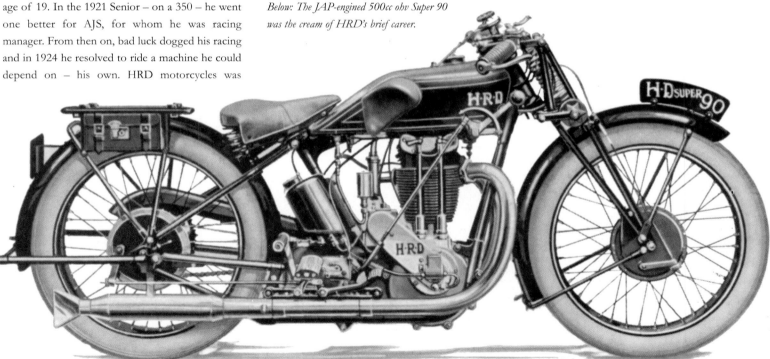

James

'THE FAMOUS James' was another enterprise founded as a Black Country bicycle company, by Harry James in 1890. Like so many others, their earliest motorcycles employed Belgian Minerva and FN engines.

The first in-house engine arrived in 1908 under the direction of Fred Kimberley. These machines also featured advanced internally-expanding (drum) brakes and stub axles – what we today call single-siders. As well as a 297cc stroker, there were four-stroke singles and V-twins in side-valve and ohv configuration. The 496cc twin, in particular, became renowned for its smoothness and easy power. It continued in one form or another for many years, even leading to a speedway derivative in the late Twenties. In the same period, James gained

Above: By the time this sturdy Captain was built in 1959, James was known only for plain but rugged runabouts – a far cry from the era of the 350SS (below) built as James were gearing up for Bert Kapshaw's victory in the 1929 Belgian Grand Prix.

their biggest road-race success when Bert Kapshaw won the 1929 175cc Belgian GP.

The GP machine was powered by a 172cc Villiers engine, one of thousands the company would use over the next 35 years. Nonetheless James clung on for a time manufacturing their own engines (in 1931 James took over the Baker motorcycle company whose founder had created the first Villiers engines), but by 1946 their range was entirely fitted with bought-in Villiers powerplants. Models such as the 197cc 8E and later Commodores, Cadets and Captains earned a reputation for ruggedness, and trials machines like the Cotswold enjoyed competition success. In 1947 they had joined Francis-Barnett under the AMC umbrella, for a time using poorly-built AMC engines rather than Villiers. Both companies folded in 1964. An ironic postscript is that in 1963 James formed a company to import Suzuki motorcycles, a venture forestalled by the crash of AMC.

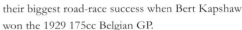

Matchless

FOUNDED IN 1899, Matchless became one of the giants, having had the priceless distinction of winning its inaugural TT through co-founder Charlie Collier, with brother Harry winning two years later and Charlie winning again in 1910. In the same year Charlie posted a prodigious 91.37mph (147.04km/h) over the standing mile on a 998cc JAP-engined V-twin. Ironically racing soon became a secondary consideration, so that even in the Thirties their racers were essentially stripped-down roadsters such as the 347cc cammy single. Their next IoM victory did not come until the Historic TT of 1984, when Dave Roper became the first American TT winner.

The 1907 TT winner was a 432cc ohv single, and singles were always the bread-and-butter heart of the pre-Second World War Matchless range. But they were perhaps best known for grandly-equipped V-twins ranging from 496 to almost 1000cc. Indeed their quality was such that Matchless supplied engines to Brough-Superior, Morgan cars, Coventry Eagle, OEC and elsewhere.

1931 saw the acquisition of AJS from the Stevens brothers, uniting production at their plant in Plumstead, south-east London. (The company also bought Sunbeam in 1936, but sold it on to BSA shortly after.) Initially the 'Ajay' and 'Matchbox' ranges maintained a separate identity, but gradually

A duo of post-war Matchless twins. The 498cc G9 (above) first arrived in 1949 and led ultimately to production of the 646cc G12 (left).

converged so that in the post-war era there was little to chose between them. By this time the enterprise had become AMC – Associated Motor Cycles – swallowing up Francis-Barnett, James and Norton in turn. The post-war Matchless range comprised ohv four-stroke singles and parallel twins, the latter beginning with the 498cc G9 (AJS Model 20) of 1949, which later grew to 592 and 646cc. Biggest of all was the Norton Atlas-engined 745cc G15 (AJS Model 33) of 1964-69 (see AJS), which overlapped with the collapse of AMC and the creation of Norton Villiers in 1967.

MATCHLESS SILVER HAWK

There had been previous exceptions to the staple Matchless fare of singles and V-twins, notably a 986cc flat twin in 1916. This ambitious cammy four was another, Plumstead's spectacular response to Ariel's Square Four, with which it co-starred at the 1931 Olympia Show. Designed by the youngest Collier brother, Bert, it was partly a response to the failure of the Silver Arrow, a sophisticated narrow-angle 397cc V-twin which had excited everyone except the buying public. In essence the Hawk comprised two Arrows side-by-side, forming a 26 degree V-four with the crank across the frame. Like the Ariel, the rear cylinders were prone to overheat, and it was a less refined design, and £5 dearer. Sales were poor and it was withdrawn after 1935.

MATCHLESS MODEL X

From around 1910 to 1939, Matchless' reputation rested largely on big, relaxed V-twins. Often these were intended for sidecar use, but in 1937 the Model X was released with a new shorter frame as a solo 'Sports Tourist'. It was a high-quality device. Indeed the same 50-degree engine was employed to the same effortless effect by Brough Superior for the much more costly SS80 (its ohv brother also powered later SS100s). After the war, V-twins largely disappeared from the scene: the Model X was one of the last, and one of the best.

The 592cc Silver Hawk V-four failed to match the sustained appeal of Ariel's Square Four.

SPECIFICATION	MATCHLESS SILVER HAWK
ENGINE	air-cooled 592cc sohc V-four
POWER	N/A
TRANSMISSION	4-speed
FUEL TANK	3.25 gallons (14.8 litres)
WEIGHT	380lb (172kg)
TOP SPEED	80mph (129km/h)

Right: This handsome Seeley-framed G50 already has one Classic Manx GP win and is the epitome of the modern classic racer.

MATCHLESS G50

When the classic 500cc Matchless racing single replaced the twin-cylinder G45 in 1959, the reign of the four-stroke single was already over. But the Matchless was never envisaged as a grand prix winner. It was popular because the 47bhp, Jack Williams-designed single, a derivative of the 350cc AJS 7R, was a true over-the-counter racer, competitive enough straight out of the crate, and far simpler to maintain than Norton's Manx. The aim was simple: a practicable racing machine at an affordable price. It wasn't until Colin Seeley began making special frames that the Matchless regularly began to blow off the 500 Manx. Indeed the G50 has never won a truly competitive grand prix, its

Right: Remarkably, racing G50 engines such as this can still be built from brand-new parts.

three successes – at Finland in 1962, Argentina in 1961 and '62 – coming in the absence of the prevailing Hondas and MVs.

SPECIFICATION	MATCHLESS SEELEY G50
ENGINE	air-cooled 496cc sohc single
POWER	47bhp @ 6500rpm
TRANSMISSION	5- or 6-speed
FUEL TANK	various
WEIGHT	276lb (125kg)
TOP SPEED	80mph (129km/h)

New Imperial

IN THE 36 years of its existence, 1903 to 1939, New Imperial built some of the prettiest and most technically interesting machines, and for a time were a dominant force in British racing. Although mainly associated with light- and middleweight singles, in their formative years the company used bought-in engines of 246 to 996cc, principally from Precision (later Beardmore Precision) and JAP. 1922 brought the company its first competition 'success' when a 348cc JAP New

Above: A very rare 1934 497cc V-twin, raced from 1933-5. Some examples were supercharged.

Imp set the fastest lap in the Lightweight TT at 56.46mph (90.86km/h). The rider that day was the great Bert le Vack, responsible for designing both the Junior engine and its 248cc Lightweight counterpart. Although fast, neither proved very reliable.

Two years later, however, Eddie Twemlow made amends with a spectacular double in the Junior and Lightweight races, also taking the 250cc race in 1925. In 1926 New Imperial began manufacturing its own engines at the Birmingham factory, consolidating a range of solid if unremarkable single-cylinder roadsters of both ohv and side-valve design, culminating in such machines as the 350cc Blue Prince.

However, in 1932 – ironically as the Depression was biting – it embarked on a wholesale programme of unit-construction engines. This relatively novel layout, in which the engine and gearbox are fabricated as a 'unit' and linked by helical gears, is far superior to 'non-unit' construction, notwithstanding the fact that it was not widespread until the Sixties. The first such machine was the Unit Minor 150, which boasted fully enclosed valvegear, as well. This was followed in 1933 by the 250 Unit Super, 350 Unit Plus and the 80mph (129km/h), 500cc Unit Major. By 1938 practically the entire range of over 20 models was 'Unit'. 1938 also marked the introduction of rear suspension, using a triangulated pivot, after the Vincent fashion.

Above: The twin left was essentially two of these 250cc factory engines united on a common crankcase.

Not so with the racers, at least initially. These were all exquisitely built, but were non-unit. Most remarkable were the 497cc V-twins, for which Len Horton effectively joined two singles on a common crankcase, including some in supercharged form. Ridden by Horton and 'Ginger' Wood, they were very fast and reputedly terrifying over the bumps at Brooklands. Nonetheless, Wood became the first rider of a British multi to cover over 100 miles (161km) in a single hour.

In 1932 Leo Davenport had brought New Imperial another Lightweight TT win, followed by Charlie Dobson's second place a year later. But arguably their finest hour came in the 1936

Above: A spring frame roadster 500cc single built in 1938, the year before New Imp's demise.

Lightweight TT when Bob Foster rode the last British four-stroke to win the event – at record speed, by a margin of fully five minutes. A further measure of Foster's achievement was that the little machine was notionally obsolete in other ways: normally-aspirated, rigid framed, and with a mere two valves operated by pushrods. Designed around the Unit Super 250 by Matt Wright, it was hoped that roadster sales would improve on the back of

the TT success, but sadly, it was not to be. The following year illness brought the death of New Imperial's driving force, Norman Downs, and Wright soon moved to AJS. The company continued to slide until swallowed up by Jack Sangster's Ariel/Triumph in 1939.

SPECIFICATION	NEW IMPERIAL UNIT SUPER 250 (ROADSTER)
ENGINE	air-cooled 247cc ohv single
POWER	N/A
TRANSMISSION	4-speed
FUEL TANK	2.75 gallons (12.5 litres)
WEIGHT	N/A
TOP SPEED	61mph (98km/h)

Norton

ALTHOUGH NEVER a huge company, decades of Norton racing successes have given the company a unique place in British motorcycle history. Founded by James Lansdowne 'Pa' Norton in 1898, the Norton Manufacturing Company initially made bicycle components, producing its first powered two-wheeler in 1902. Early models used engines by Moto-Rêve and Peugeot, and in 1907 privateer Rem Fowler took one of the latter to victory in the twin cylinder class of the inaugural Isle of Man TT. It was to be the first of many famous victories all over the world.

Encouraged by this success, 'Pa' Norton designed the first in-house engine, a 633cc side-valve single called the 'Big Four' (it had a nominal 4hp) which was to remain in production in one form or another for almost 50 years. In 1911 this was joined by a 490cc stablemate, tuned 'BRS' versions of which were good for 70mph (113km/h) and prospered at Brooklands, despite being belt-driven and single speed.

In 1922 Norton's first overhead valver, the Model 18, appeared. Within two years it had achieved another notable TT success, now on the gruelling Mountain Circuit, when Alec Bennett took the Senior at an average of 61.64mph (99.2km/h) and George Tucker the sidecar race at 51.31mph (82.57km/h).

Sadly, Norton's founder died one year later and so failed to witness the first of a dynasty of overhead-cam racers bearing his name on which Bennett again conquered the TT. This milestone was designed by Tucker's passenger from the 1924 TT, Walter Moore, a former Douglas technician. When he left the Bracebridge Street company, Arthur Carrol took over the 'cammy' mantle, replacing Moore's CS1 design with a more advanced version which was to become the immortal Manx. Under the shrewd supervision of race boss Joe Craig, factory versions of the cammy Norton went on to win seven Senior TTs in the Thirties, raising the lap record from 76 (122km/h) to over 90mph (145km/h) in the process. 350cc versions of the same engine won from 1931 to '37 inclusive.

As with Velocette – Norton's great TT rivals in the Thirties – race success was to some extent achieved at the expense of showroom models. The ohv roadsters were strong, true, but had the spark of the cammy racers only by association. After the war, even the racers were far outclassed for power by the new Italian fours, and only the peerless handling bestowed after 1950 by the McCandless brothers' twin loop Featherbed frame kept them competitive.

Mating this chassis with the new, Bert Hopwood-designed twin-cylinder ohv engine would

Left: The classic British racing single: Norton's 500 'Manx'. 'Garden Gate' plunger frame and telescopic forks mark it as from the late Forties.

ultimately produce one of the finest roadsters ever to leave Norton's gates. But when the Dominator first appeared in 1948, it was in a rigid frame. The first Featherbed-equipped Dominator 88 de Luxe was first shown at Earls Court in 1951, but was for export only. As an interim measure, Bob Collier grafted swinging-arm rear ends onto their old lugged frames, which were rushed into the range for 1953.

Eventually the Featherbed became Norton's standard frame, the yardstick by which the handling of other machinery was judged long after

Above: A Dominator '99' from 1958, by which time the Featherbed frame was standard across the range. Right: A Ray Petty 500 Manx. Its lightweight frame kept it competitive well into the Sixties.

production ceased in the late Sixties. In late 1955 the 600cc Dominator 99 was added to its 500cc stablemate. The bigger engine was, like all subsequent Nortons, non-unit. It developed 31bhp at 5750rpm – an improvement, but significantly less than Triumph's sporting twin. In 1960 a revised Featherbed, the 'Slimline' was introduced.

Yet these were troubled times for Norton which in 1962 was absorbed into the AMC Group, partly as a result of the failure of their smaller new models, the 250cc Jubilee and 350cc Navigator twins. The 750cc Norton Atlas appeared on the home market two years later, the same engine appearing as the Matchless G15 under the AMC flag. But two years later still AMC themselves collapsed into liquidation. Norton Villiers arose from that particular pile of ashes, and with them, the next generation of Norton vertical twins.

Norton's new base was Andover in Hampshire, where in early 1967 a replacement for the 650 and 750cc twins was designed under a team led by Dr. Stefan Bauer. The result was the Commando, which not only wore its cylinders inclined at a new, rakish angle, but – after the violent shakes of the 750 Atlas – featured a unique form of 'Isolastic' anti-vibration measure as well.

Although sometimes considered a débâcle, Commando production accounted for more machines than all other post-war Norton twins

combined and it was voted *Motor Cycle News* 'Machine of the Year' on five consecutive occasions. But by the time production ceased in mid-'77, no adequate replacement was on the horizon. Norton went on to produce a range of rotary-engined models on a very small scale in the Eighties, limping from crisis to financial crisis in the process. Despite some heroic racing successes – notably Steve Hislop's 1992 Senior win, still the fastest ever TT race – it was a forlorn end for one of the greatest names in motorcycling.

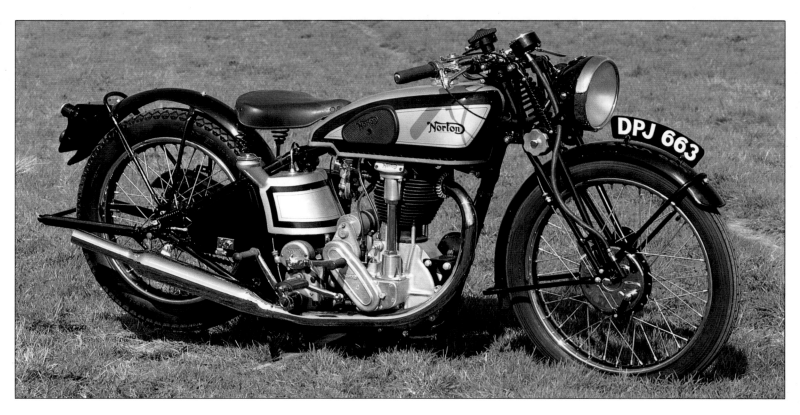

Left: A 1937 Norton Model 30 'International', the road-going equivalent of the glorious Manx.

SPECIFICATION	NORTON MODEL 30 INTERNATIONAL
ENGINE	air-cooled 490cc ohc single
POWER	29.5bhp @ 5500rpm
TRANSMISSION	4-speed
FUEL TANK	3.75 gallons (17 litres)
WEIGHT	380lb (172kg)
TOP SPEED	95mph (153km/h) up to 120mph (193km/h) in racing trim)

NORTON INTERNATIONAL

In a book of classic machines, the 'Inter' must be rated more classic than most, being one of very few roadsters whose full sister was not only a thoroughbred racing machine, but the most successful racer ever produced in the UK. Essentially, this was a 'cammy' Manx with lights.

First offered to the public in 1932, the Model 30 500cc Inter was at once tested at a startling 100mph (161km/h), a speed only previously attained by machines twice as big. (There was also a 350cc Model 40 Inter.) Not surprisingly, the Inter became the most desirable sporting machine of the pre-war era.

Despite the adoption of telescopic forks, and later full Featherbed swinging arm frame, after the Second World War the Inter didn't have things all its own way. The 497cc Dominator launched in 1948 offered a comparable level of performance in a machine that was far cleaner, easier to maintain, and cheaper to produce. Stripped-down Inters were still popular amongst racing privateers, but even here a threat was looming with BSA's equally legendary Gold Star. After 1958 one of the greats quietly

Above: By 1952 the Inter had plunger rear suspension, although the Featherbed would soon take its place.

Above: Inter's bevel-driven cam design is clearly evident on this example. Note flat-slide carb without air cleaner.

45

NORTON 650SS

Although Norton's 'cooking' twins were always well thought of, it was not until the unveiling of the 650SS in 1960 that the company truly had a rival to the fastest sports models from Triumph. The 650SS (a 500cc version, the 88SS followed one year later) was truly a dream machine: Norton's best-ever engine in the best chassis on earth.

The SS featured a Model 99 engine enlarged from 597 to 646cc by a 7mm longer stroke. With an additional boost from twin carbs, power rose prodigiously from 31 to 49bhp. Happily this proved to be the ideal maximum size for Hopwood's twin, for vibration from the later 750cc Atlas was to prove diabolical. But most of all, the SS had the McCandless brothers' bronze-welded Featherbed chassis (now in waisted 'Slimline' form) and 'Roadholder' forks. This was a street bike – and a fast one – which handled better than many pure racing machines.

With comparable products already available from BSA, Royal Enfield, AJS/Matchless and Triumph (the Bonneville had arrived in '59), the SS had to be good – and it was. Early versions suffered some failures – notably burst cylinder barrels and

fatigue fractures of various fittings – but through it all shone that pedigree handling package. Ridden to the limit, no other production machine could come close. And with a top speed of around 113mph (182km/h), and standing quarter times in the sixes, the new Norton was no slouch on the straights. Not surprisingly, the 650SS went on to win production races by the score.

Below: Perhaps the finest Norton roadster of the post-war years, a 1966 650SS.

NORTON COMMANDO

The Commando, in 745 and later 829cc form, was the final development of the archetypal British vertical twin. Essentially it was a solution to the fearful vibration of the Atlas engine – the 'Isolastic' system, in which the engine and transmission, including the swing-arm, were isolated from the rest of the machine by a sophisticated form of rubber mounting. When introduced in 1967 it boasted 9bhp more than its predecessor, with 'Combat' engined versions claiming yet 7bhp more.

SPECIFICATION	NORTON 650SS
ENGINE	air-cooled 647cc ohv vertical twin
POWER	49bhp @ 6800rpm
TRANSMISSION	4-speed
FUEL TANK	3.5 gallons (16 litres)
WEIGHT	410lb (186kg)
TOP SPEED	113mph (182km/h)

46

Dr Bauer's anti-vibration system worked astonishingly well, and a new adjustment system on the 850 Mk.2A made maintenance far simpler. If the Commando had a weakness – and it did – it was its crankshaft, especially on the highly-stressed 65bhp 'Combat' engine. Although this and head-lifting problems were later solved, the Commando's reputation was tarnished.

Yet in many ways the Commando was the best of the vertical twins, a handsome device with a strong, punchy power delivery, equally good on long runs and along tight back-roads. The 850 Commando appeared in 1973, and a more refined electric-start Mk.2A 850 a year later. For many, this was the last 'true' Norton.

Right: One of the very first, Woolwich-built Commandos, a 750 Fastback from 1968. Production was soon to move to Andover, Hampshire.

Left: By the time this example was built in 1974 the Commando had grown to 829cc. Note disc front brake and more conventional styling. Despite the extra capacity, reliability was now much improved.

SPECIFICATION	NORTON COMMANDO 750 NORTON COMMANDO 850
ENGINE	air-cooled 745cc (829cc) ohv vertical twin
POWER	58bhp @ 6800rpm (58bhp @ 5900rpm)
TRANSMISSION	4-speed
FUEL TANK	3 or 5.5 gallons (13.6 or 25 litres)
WEIGHT	430lb (195kg)
TOP SPEED	110-120mph (177-193km/h)

OEC

THE OSBORN Engineering Company, to give it its full title, began powered life like so many other pioneers with imported Minerva engines. But it was not until John Osborn took over from founding father Frederick that they began to establish a reputation, in around 1920. A year later they took over the manufacture of Blackburne motorcycles and engines, briefly taking the name OEC-Blackburne. Their larger models favoured large V-twin JAP engines. In the later Thirties they were also responsible for JAP-engined Atlanta-Duo singles built in their home town of Portsmouth.

OEC were best-known for their roadsters' curious 'duplex' steering system, designed by Fred Wood. Other OEC oddities included a 998cc sidecar outfit with a steering wheel. The duplex system was heavy but far stiffer than girder forks, giving unparalleled stability and some of the advantages associated with more complex hub-centre designs. Indeed it was used on Joe Wright's 137.23mph (220.84km/h) JAP-engined supercharged record breaker at Arpajon, France in 1930. The company was no stranger to speed, for four years earlier Claude Temple had taken his OEC-Temple to a world record of 121.3mph (195.2km/h) at the same venue.

Yet ironically, OEC was renowned for the excellence of its chassis rather than its powerplants. However, by the late Thirties one of the best-known models, the Matchless-engined 500

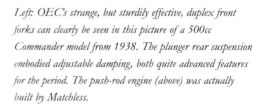

Commander, was capable of over 80mph (129km/h). Unusually for its time, it also featured plunger-type rear suspension with adjustable damping. After the Second World War OEC's fortunes faded – one of their premier models was the inaptly-named Apollo, a 250cc side-valve single – and motorcycle production ceased in 1954.

Left: OEC's strange, but sturdily effective, duplex front forks can clearly be seen in this picture of a 500cc Commander model from 1938. The plunger rear suspension embodied adjustable damping, both quite advanced features for the period. The push-rod engine (above) was actually built by Matchless.

SPECIFICATION	1938 OEC COMMANDER
ENGINE	air-cooled 498cc ohv single
POWER	N/A
TRANSMISSION	4-speed
FUEL TANK	3 gallons (13.6 litres)
WEIGHT	N/A
TOP SPEED	82mph (132km/h)

OK Supreme

OK BECAME Supreme only in 1927, and to prove the point Frank Longman won the Lightweight TT one year later. Founded as bicycle makers Humphrey and Dawes in 1882, the name 'Supreme' was added when Dawes to left to concentrate very successfully on pedal-powered products. The duo had dabbled with de Dion- and Minerva-engined motorcycles since 1899, but not until after 1910 were they serious manufacturers.

A racing fanatic, Ernie Humphries first took his OK-Precision to the TT in 1912, earning third place on the lightweight event. 1913 brought a 346cc liquid-cooled Green engine and one of the company's very few twins, powered by a fore-and aft ABC boxer engine. After the First World War, their own two-stroke complemented Blackburne-engined models of 247 and 347cc, and later oil-cooled Bradshaw and JAP engines.

In 1922 the 18 year-old prodigy Wal Handley set the fastest Lightweight TT lap on a 250 OK-Blackburne, won the Ulster GP, then set the fastest TT lap again in 1923 before crashing.

The 1928 TT-winning machine used a proprietary ohv JAP engine, albeit with a special cylinder head, but in 1930 OK's masterpiece

Above: Surely one of the prettiest of racers, this OK Supreme 250cc cammy single dates from 1934.

appeared. The TT30 'Lighthouse' was a bevel-drive ohc 250 (later also 350) designed by George Jones and Ray Mason and built for OK in Gloucester. However, it was expensive to produce, and the company later reverted to a simpler ohc design (which was to dominate grass-track for years) and cheaper JAP-engined models of 250 to 350cc. Shortly before the outbreak of war a utilitarian 250 side-valve, the 10bhp SV/39 also appeared. It was effectively to be OK Supreme's final model. Ernie's son John built a few JAP-engined grass-trackers in 1946 but was killed shortly after and production died with him.

Left: A 250cc 'Lighthouse' Model TT/30 roadster built in 1932. The elaborate engine was later replaced by simpler ohc designs, similar to the racer above.

P&M

PHELON AND Moore, more than any other British manufacturer, found a formula they liked and stuck with it, come what may. To every motorcyclist, mention of the word 'Panther' conveys images of big, slow-revving 'sloper' singles which proverbially fired every other lamp post.

In 1900, founder Joah Phelon's very first design was essentially of this type, using the forward-sloping engine in place of front down tubes, a radical but clever innovation. The design was sold to Humber, for which Phelon received royalties of 7s 6d per machine. Phelon and business partner Harry Rayner continued to build a few machines in their Cleckheaton engineering shop. Then, following the death of Rayner, Phelon joined forces with Richard Moore and in 1904 P&M was formed.

The basic model was always a big single, initially of 500cc, which acquired a two-speed gearbox, forks, brakes and so on as the technology developed. The First World War interrupted development of a V-twin, with the engine, of course, a frame member, much in the manner of Series C Vincents. 1923 brought first a side-valve four-speeder of 555cc, and then an ohv 500 designed by Granville Bradshaw: the first machine to be dubbed Panther. Although already associated with sidecar-lugging machines, P&M dabbled in TT racing in the mid-Twenties, their best result being a fourth for Tommy Bullus in the 1925 Senior. They also enjoyed some success in trials, and in the late Twenties would even make speedway machines, but P&M rarely laboured under expensive sporting pretensions.

Two years later the 'Panthette' followed – a surprising departure as this was a unit-construction 250cc V-twin, with transverse cylinders, like a modern Moto Guzzi. It was not a success, and a range of Villiers-engined two-strokes was created to soak up the Panthette's unneeded spares inventory. In 1929 the Panther was enlarged to 598cc. This was followed by the 250cc Model 20 which might have prospered had the Depression not intervened. Instead, a deal was struck to supply London dealers Pride and Clarke with a special bargain-basement 250, the Red Panther, at less than £30. It was certainly cheap, pretty nasty, but – typical P&M – surprisingly indestructible, even winning the Maudes Trophy in 1934.

As the economy improved, so did the Cleckheaton range, with ohv Redwing singles of 350 (based on the Red Panther) and 500cc, and the

Left: During the Depression this 250cc Model 20 begat the notorious 'Red Panther' which, despite shameless cost-cutting, proved as cheerfully indestructible as practically every other P&M model.

SPECIFICATION	P&M PANTHER 120S
ENGINE	air-cooled 645cc ohv sloper single
POWER	28bhp @ 4500rpm
TRANSMISSION	4-speed
FUEL TANK	3 gallons (13.6 litres)
WEIGHT	426lb (193kg)
TOP SPEED	80mph (129km/h)

Left: By the time this 120S was produced in 1964 the classic Panther single had grown to a whopping 645cc, with a piston stroke of well over 4in (102mm). Below: The reason for the 'sloper' appellation can clearly be seen in the disposition of the cylinder barrel of this 598cc Model 100 from 1950.

598cc Model 100. After the Second World War, as if recognizing that there was more to motorcycling than big singles, P&M continued to strive for acceptable new models. There were new, non-sloper singles of 250 and 350cc, and an early two-stroke scooter, the Princess.

Yet despite a further interlude with Villiers-engined two-strokes (one of which, a 250 twin, boasted a 'Dynastart' electric foot), throughout all these years the heart of the range remained the big sloper single. By 1964 this had grown to no less than 645cc: the £267 Model 120. For all its lusty virtues, this was essentially a 60-year-old design, economical but slow, and increasingly irrelevant to motorcycle buyers. Despite the efforts of yet another Pride and Clarke Red Panther, now a quite striking 250cc two-stroke twin, sales gradually declined and two-wheeler production ceased in 1967.

Rex

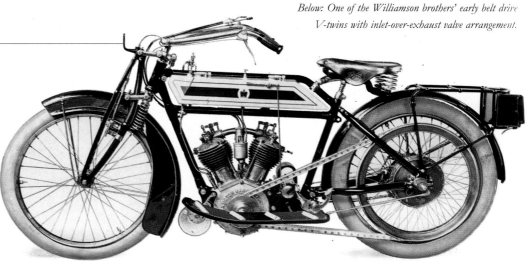

REX (later Rex-Acme) was one of the jewels of the early British motorcycle scene. Beginning as car manufacturers in Coventry in 1899, the Williamson brothers, Billy and Harold, soon produced motorcycles with their own single and twin-cylinder power units, notably a 456cc side-valve and 726cc ioe V-twin. Vibrant and innovative, they produced the first telescopic forks in 1906 (helping Billy Heaton to third place in the first TT) and a 470cc two-stroke racing twin. Despite this, the duo was ousted from the company in 1911, although the irrepressible Billy subsequently created the Williamson, a 1000cc liquid-cooled flat twin.

Under new boss George Hemingway, Rex continued to make their own engines, also producing a separate range of Rex-JAP machines

for nearby Premier. A sophisticated all-chain-drive 952cc was aborted with the outbreak of war. In 1919 they took over neighbours Coventry-Acme,

Below: A 348cc Blackburne-engined 'Speed King' of the late Twenties. Wal Handley's TT exploits gave such sports models a lively boost, but it would not last.

adopting the name Rex-Acme two years later as the company entered its prime. By 1926 the range included at least 15 models ranging from a 172cc Villiers to a 746cc JAP V-twin.

Much of their greatness derived from one man, Wal Handley. The precocious young Brummie had first shown his mettle for OK at the 1922 and '23 TTs. By the end of June he was a Rex-Acme rider, romping to victory in the Belgian and Ulster GPs. Two years later he recorded the first ever TT double in winning the Lightweight and Junior events, adding the Lightweight again in 1927 (Rex was rarely a force in the larger class, where it campaigned a 498cc ohv V-twins in 1926). However, by this time sales were sliding disastrously; in 1932 the company was taken over by a sidecar manufacturer, Mills-Fulford, who dropped motorcycle production the following year.

Rickman Interceptor

THE INTERCEPTOR was one of the better consequences of bankruptcy. When Royal Enfield went out of business in 1968, 200 Series II Constellation engines were left stranded en route to Indian in the USA. The result was the Interceptor, an amalgam of Rickman's acknowledged chassis know-how and Enfield's biggest twin.

Founded in 1959, Hampshire-based Rickman were chiefly renowned for their off-road machines, but soon developed a reputation for high-quality roadster and racing frames. The Interceptor's Métisse chassis was designed to offer 'extreme rigidity with minimum weight', and was superbly executed. The finished bike cost £550 and weighed just 353lb (160kg), fully 95lb (43kg) less than a standard Constellation. The quality of the components, including Rickman's own forks and some of the first modern disc brakes, encouraged a French magazine to call this 'the Rolls-Royce of motorcycles'.

Power came from the 736cc high-cam Constellation engine, sitting 'semi-unit' with its gearbox. Hugely tractable, it was good for around 115mph (185km/h). Low and lean, it combined stability with agility to an unprecedented degree. In 1970 British machines such as this could still set a new standard in handling which it would take the Japanese over a decade to match. Indeed, the same frame was later to house big Honda and Kawasaki fours. In showing that even big bikes could handle, the Interceptor paved the way for the rest.

Below: The Interceptor proved a remarkable salvage operation, turning bankrupt stock into one of the finest-handling classic British bikes. Note the very early disc brakes, and curious mounting of the rider's footrests — actually welded to the exhaust pipes.

SPECIFICATION	RICKMAN INTERCEPTOR
ENGINE	air-cooled 736cc ohv vertical twin
POWER	56bhp @ 6750rpm
TRANSMISSION	4-speed
FUEL TANK	4 gallons (18.2 litres)
WEIGHT (dry)	353lb (160kg)
TOP SPEED	115mph (185km/h)

53

Royal Enfield

ANOTHER COMPANY with its roots in bicycle manufacturing, Enfield – the 'Royal' came later – was founded in Redditch, Worcestershire in 1897, by Albert Eadie and Robert Smith. Their first powered machines were a De Dion-engined trike produced in 1899, and later a single with a 211cc Minerva engine similar to Triumph's first model. They then appeared to lose interest in two-wheelers, going broke with the Enfield Autocar, before Smith's gaze returned to motorcycles again in 1910. The emphasis now was on V-twins, first a Motosacoche-powered solo, then the famous Model 180, a big 770cc JAP-engined sidecar-hauler (a descendant of which carried a Vickers machine gun during the First World War). Another V-twin followed in 1913, a beautiful 425cc solo. A squad of eight of these, sleeved down to 347cc, contested the 1914 TT in which the best finished a worthy third.

After hostilities had ceased, Enfield continued to concentrate on twins, although they enjoyed some success with a 225cc single which had appeared shortly before the war. In 1921 the biggest twin grew to 976cc, now of Enfield's own design. This was followed by a lively JAP-engined 350cc single, available in both ohv and side-valve form. The latter began a strong tradition of Enfield trials success.

SPECIFICATION	ROYAL ENFIELD CONSTELLATION (INTERCEPTOR)
ENGINE	air-cooled 692cc (736cc) ohv vertical twin
POWER	51bhp @ 6250rpm (56bhp @ 6750rpm)
TRANSMISSION	4-speed
FUEL TANK	4.5 gallons (20.5 litres) (3 gallons/13.6 litres)
WEIGHT (dry)	410lb (186kg) (375lb/170kg)
TOP SPEED	112mph (180km/h) (115mph/185km/h)

The first Enfield big single, a 488cc side-valver, arrived in 1927, followed two years later by an ohv derivative. The first ohv Bullets followed in 1930, eventually in 250, 350 and 500cc form, along with quite a sophisticated 150cc lightweight, the Model X. Throughout all this, the company rarely produced the most exotic machines – notwithstanding the four-valve JF of the Thirties – but they were often the first with more down-to-earth technology, such as cush drives and wet sump crankcases. For the most part, they changed tack from the tried-and-tested only reluctantly. They produced big side-valve V-twins like the 1140cc Model K almost until the Second World War.

During the war years themselves, Redditch's bread-and-butter military model was a 350cc side-valve single, as robust and dependable as any commander might want. But after 1945, a new generation of Enfield's was required, beginning with a 125cc two-stroke, the ohv 350cc Model G and later a 500cc version, the Model J. These latter two machines were to lead to the Bullet series of models.

Below: The biggest British twin of its era, this 692cc Royal Enfield Constellation dates from 1960. The design dated from the earlier Meteor models.

But what Enfield knew it needed most of all was a flagship model, and V-twins were now (temporarily) consigned to history: it had to be a four-stroke vertical twin in the mould of Edward Turner's Triumph. But those produced in Redditch would be bigger, and bigger – in America, at least – was best. Their first attempt was the 500cc Meteor of 1948, which set the pattern with a one-piece iron crankshaft, separate heads and barrels, and dry-sump oiling, but with the oil neatly contained in a reservoir cast integrally with the crankcases. The Meteor also boasted swing-arm rear suspension at a time when BSA, Norton and Triumph were still persevering with plunger rear ends.

Feedback from the US market prompted the development of a larger machine, and in 1953 the 692cc Meteor was the result. From the Meteor was derived the Super Meteor, then in 1958 the more sporting Constellation. It was fast – independently timed at 112mph (180km/h) – and far less revvy than any Triumph twin. The threat of excessive vibration was reduced by dynamic balancing of the crankshafts, a feature unique to RE.

Constellation production continued until 1962 and the introduction of the 736cc Interceptor, followed by a revised Mk2 Interceptor, but neither was very successful and the company collapsed in 1968, stranding a shipment of engines en route to the USA. These were subsequently used in the exquisite Rickman Interceptor.

350 BULLET

Although the Bullet name had figured in Redditch lore since 1930, the version introduced in 1949 is the most familiar. An alloy-headed variant of the old

Above: The only classic 'British' bike still in production, this 500cc Bullet was built in Madras. The Indian Enfield factory – minus the 'Royal' – originally built machines under licence but outlived the parent company.

55

SPECIFICATION	ROYAL ENFIELD 350 BULLET
ENGINE	air-cooled 346cc ohv single
POWER	18bhp @ 5750rpm
TRANSMISSION	4-speed
FUEL TANK	3.75 gallons (17 litres)
WEIGHT (dry)	350lb (159kg)
TOP SPEED	75mph (121km/h)

Model G, this was the first British model to feature full swing-arm suspension. Early examples were used in trials, but as a roadster it offered economy, good comfort and handling, lively performance and, above all, durability. In the Fifties Bullets began to be built under licence in Madras, India, where Enfield manufacturing continues today.

Above: A 'genuine' Redditch 350cc Bullet from 1955.

CONTINENTAL GT

The five-speed GT, Enfield's most sporting four-stroke lightweight of the Sixties, was the final development of the Crusader and Super-5 series. Complete with racing-type fairing, 'bum-stop' seat and elegant clean lines, it was almost a BSA Gold Star in miniature. And, with almost twice the power of the first Crusader, it was no slouch. The great Geoff Duke even ran a GT race squad, although the machine was no match for Enfield's two-stroke

56

SPECIFICATION	ROYAL ENFIELD CONTINENTAL GT
ENGINE	air-cooled 248cc ohv single
POWER	21bhp @ 7500rpm
TRANSMISSION	5-speed
FUEL TANK	3.5 gallons (16 litres)
WEIGHT (dry)	300lb (136kg)
TOP SPEED	84mph (135km/h)

GP5. Like much else on offer from the British industry at the time, however, the little Enfield was no match for the wave of new sports lightweights arriving from Japan. Motorcycle production ceased after 1966.

Opposite and below: The Continental GT was a laudable Enfield attempt to create a sort of lightweight, budget BSA Gold Star. Despite striking looks and brisk performance, it succumbed to the entry of more sophisticated sports machines into the UK market.

57

Rudge

ALTHOUGH COMMONLY known by the first part of their full company title, Rudge-Whitworth, the man whose name it was died in 1880, long before the company's first motorcycle. Dan Rudge was a Wolverhampton innkeeper who also built bicycles. After his death the bicycle company was sold, to George Woodcock, in 1885, finding a home (with several other Woodcock companies) at the same premises in Crow Road, Coventry which had housed Ariel's sewing machine business. After the death of Woodcock, the company was acquired by Whitworth Cycles, so forming Rudge-Whitworth in 1894.

It was another 17 years before the first Rudge motorcycle, an inlet-over-exhaust single of 500cc, went on sale (although the company had already sold re-badged French Werner machines). Rudges immediately did well in competition, setting records over one hour (first machine over 60mph [96km/h]) and at Brooklands circuit. Tragically their 1911 Isle of Man ambitions ended when Vic Surridge became the first TT fatality.

Perhaps the most famous Rudge of the pre-war years, until production ceased in 1923, was the Multi. Previous standard Rudges had been single speed, but the Multi, introduced in 1912, used a variable belt-drive system not unlike that seen 60 years later on Daf cars. Offering a notional 20 speeds, any doubts about the system's performance were assuaged when C.G. Pullin brought Rudge their first Senior TT win in 1914, covering 225 miles (362km) at an average of 49.5mph (79.7km/h). The multi gear was later fitted to other models, including the 998cc 'Multwin' of 1919.

After the war Rudge's range expanded under the careful direction of John V. Pugh, but it was not until the late Twenties that the glory years returned with a new range of four-valve singles designed by Fred Anstey. In 1928 Graham Walker (father of Formula 1 motor-racing commentator Murray) took one to victory in the 500cc Ulster grand prix, the first race ever to be won at a speed of 80mph (129km/h). The 'Ulster' name was to grace sporting Rudges for the next decade.

Further success followed under the shrewd direction of race boss George Hack: a Junior/Senior TT double in 1931; one year later a new four-valve 250 Rudge scored a TT 1-2-4 straight off the drawing board. Three years later it did better still with a 1-2-3.

But on public roads the £85 500cc Ulster was king – a close brother of the racers, with a radial four-valve cylinder head and a top speed over 90mph (145km/h). The cycle parts, and particularly the huge, interconnected eight-inch (20cm) brakes, were similarly advanced. For £7 less the 'cooking'

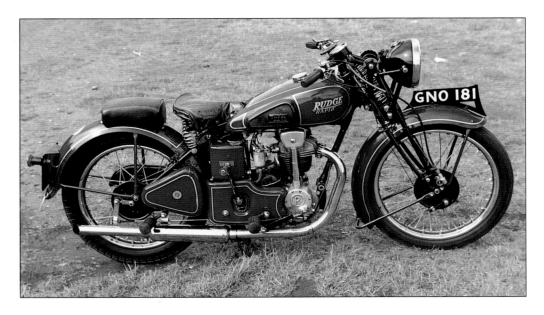

Left: As well as their better-known 500cc models, Rudge produced potent quarter-litre machines such as this 1937 245cc Rapid. Over 50 years later, similar models continued to prosper in vintage racing.

The legendary 'Ulster' was the pinnacle of road-going Rudges. By 1937 (below) the exposed valves of the 1935 example (left) had become enclosed, but the pedigree was the same. The front and rear brakes were linked, as Moto Guzzi's were to become more than 40 years later, and top-of-the-range Hondas only recently. Capable of a genuine 90mph (145km/h) in street trim, this was the fastest 500cc machine of its day, bar the far more expensive Norton International.

SPECIFICATION	RUDGE ULSTER
ENGINE	air-cooled 499cc ohv four-valve single
POWER	around 28bhp @ 5200rpm
TRANSMISSION	4-speed
FUEL TANK	3.5 gallons (16 litres)
WEIGHT (dry)	298lb (135kg)
TOP SPEED	92mph (148km/h)

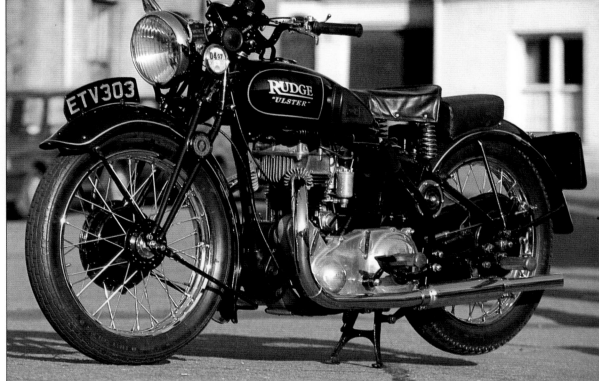

model – the 500 Special – boasted four-valve 'parallel' heads, making it easier to maintain and scarcely less desirable. Indeed, the potent four-valve engine was so desirable as to be sold widely to other manufacturers, both at home and overseas.

For all this success, Rudge suffered badly during the Depression. The race shop closed after '33 and, after a succession of abortive rescue plans, motorcycle production ceased in 1939.

Scott

ALFRED ANGAS Scott was one of the great innovators of motorcycling's early years. Scott it was who patented a form of caliper brake as early as 1897, a fully triangulated frame, rotary induction valves, unit construction, the first motorcycle kick-start and much, much more. As early as 1904 he patented his first engine – a vertical twin two-stroke, inevitably – which he fitted onto his Premier bicycle (and occasionally into a small boat, the *Petrel*).

Scott motorcycle production began in 1908, initially at the Bradford premises of the Jowett brothers, later famous for their cars. The first Scotts used a patented frame which was to survive substantially unchanged until 1930; and a new 333cc engine. This was of the same liquid-cooled, two-stroke, parallel twin-cylinder design with which the Scott name will forever be associated.

The engine shortly grew to 450cc, with later versions displacing 498 or 596cc. All were of the 'classic' Scott design, using overhung two-bearing crankshafts with the drive taken from a central flywheel. Coolant was circulated through the large honeycomb radiator (another Scott patent) by natural thermo-syphon effect, rather than pumped.

By the time the company moved into new premises at Shipley in 1912, the 'yowling two-

strokes' had a string of competition successes behind them. Scott's twins had demonstrated that the lightness and simplicity of the two-stroke twin were potent features. As well as innumerable wins in trials and hill-climbs, Scott machines won the Senior TT in 1912 and 1913.

Early Scotts used a simple but effective two-speed transmission. The first three-speeder, the legendary Flying Squirrel, appeared in 1926. This was produced in both 498 and 596cc forms. However, four years earlier Alfred Scott had died of

pneumonia at the age of just 48. With his departure much of the initiative went out of the company, which was having increasing difficulty competing with the ever-more powerful four-strokes. In 1931 the official receiver was called in.

A Liverpudlian, Albert Reynolds stepped in to save Scott, but the under-capitalized company never fully recovered. Plans for a 650cc twin never reached fruition. An even more exciting prospect, Bill Cull's three-cylinder, two-stroke design, originally of 747, later 986cc, caused a huge stir when shown at the 1934 Olympia Show. 1938 brought a 596cc Clubman's Special whose 90mph-plus (145km/h) top speed aroused considerable interest, but the war intervened.

Right: All the classic Scott features are evident in this rare 1928 three speed Super Squirrel: low, compact twin cylinder engine, honeycomb radiator, triangulated frame. Sadly, you can't hear its haunting 'yowl'.

SPECIFICATION	SCOTT MODEL 3S
ENGINE	liquid-cooled 986cc two-stroke triple
POWER	(est) 40bhp
TRANSMISSION	4-speed
FUEL TANK	3.5 gallons (16 litres)
WEIGHT (dry)	490lb (222kg)
TOP SPEED (est)	95mph (153km/h)

Left: The monstrous, ill-fated 1000cc 3S. Below: One of the last Scotts to leave Shipley, this 1950 596cc Flying Squirrel had advanced little from the much earlier example opposite.

essentially a Scott in a sophisticated racing-type Spondon chassis. Exquisite though it was, it was under-powered and expensive, and flickered only briefly.

SCOTT MODEL 3S

A remarkable failure, only eight examples of the colossal 3S were built, the first in 1936, two years after its show debut, at a huge price of £115. Fuel was carried in the 'panniers' above the rear wheel. A very similar engine was touted as a marine powerplant in 1959, but again failed to reach volume production.

Production of the 596cc rigid-framed Flying Squirrel continued after the war, initially with girder forks and later with Dowty telescopics. In 1949 coil ignition replaced the more familiar Lucas Magdyno. However, sales were poor and production ceased less than 12 months later. From 1958 Scott Swifts, basically revised Squirrel engines in a contemporary swing-arm frame, were built in small numbers. Sadly the project was short-lived, as was the later Silk,

SPECIFICATION	SCOTT SQUIRREL
ENGINE	liquid-cooled 596cc two-stroke twin
POWER	30bhp @ 5000rpm
TRANSMISSION	3-speed
FUEL TANK	2.75 gallons (12.5 litres)
WEIGHT (dry)	395lb (179kg)
TOP SPEED	84mph (135km/h)

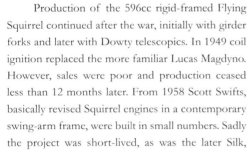

Sunbeam

WOLVERHAMPTON'S Sunbeam was ever at the swanky end of the British motorcycle scene. Founded by John Marston in 1912 – late for motorcycling, and late for him, for he was 76 years old – the company's background was in enamelware, and later bicycles and cars. The first model, designed by John Greenwood, the creator of the Imperial Rover, was a 347cc side-valve single. Although this featured an unusual engine-balancing system of eccentric flywheels, and oil-bath all-chain drive, from the outset Sunbeam was a by-word for very high quality construction and finish, rather than engineering novelty. Indeed, they were marketed as 'The Gentleman's Motor Bicycle'. A 500cc single and 770cc JAP-engined V-twin followed in 1913. Both boasted new three-speed transmissions, and did well in reliability trials. In 1914 a 500 ridden by Howard R. Davies (later of HRD fame) placed second in the Isle of Man TT.

Shortly after the outbreak of the First World War, busy with divers military contracts, Sunbeam suffered the double loss of both founder and founder's son, eventually passing to Noble Industries, which later became ICI. Far from diluting the Marston influence, this pushed Sunbeam to new heights. Their 500s won TTs in 1920, '22 and again in 1928 and '29. The first two victories were achieved by side-valve designs, the latter by an ohv machine, which had already gained considerable honours in racing and record-breaking. An ohc engine was less successful.

As the Twenties drew to a close, ICI attempted to make Sunbeam more cost- and market-conscious. The result was a smaller range: Model 9 tourer, Model 90, 492cc side-valve Lion and a new, cheap ohv 344cc model (plus the 95L racer). Worse still, quality suffered, which for many signalled the end of Marston's fine tradition, especially when the Model 90, the lasted sporting Sunbeam, was dropped in 1934. In 1936 Sunbeam changed hands again, passing to Matchless at Plumstead, whose attempts to restore the marque's former quality, in the shape of models such as the 347cc B24 and a prototype ohv V-twin, were thwarted by the outbreak of war.

As hostilities ceased, Sunbeam again changed hands, now coming under BSA's giant banner. The result was the S7, which was to be the deluxe flagship of the Small Heath range. Designed by Erling Poppe, the rubber-mounted ohc longitudinal twin had many advanced features, but sadly neither

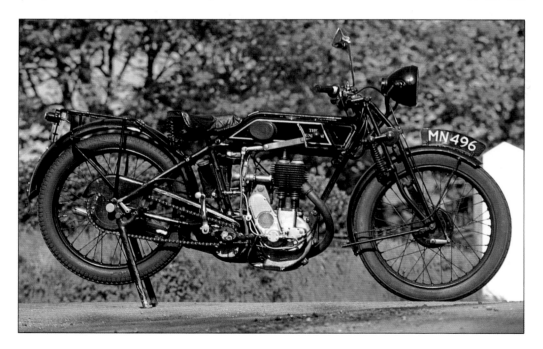

Left: A 1928 Sunbeam Model 6 side-valve. In the mid-Twenties the company was also working on overhead valve and overhead camshaft designs. The latter proved flawed, but under Graham Walker, Sunbeam achieved notable competition success with their ohv models.

SPECIFICATION	SUNBEAM S7 (S8)
ENGINE	air-cooled 487cc ohc tandem twin
POWER	25bhp @ 5800rpm (S8)
TRANSMISSION	4-speed
FUEL TANK	3.25 gallons (14.8 litres)
WEIGHT (dry)	450lb (204kg) (420lb/190kg)
TOP SPEED	78mph (126km/h) (83mph/134km/h)

Right: This 1935 Sunbeam Lion was a 492cc single derived from the famous 'longstroke' model of the Twenties. Sadly the ambitious ohc S7 (below) enjoyed nothing like the side-valve's reliability.

speed, handling nor durability were among them. The shaft final drive was particularly troublesome.

'The world's most magnificent motor cycle', went on sale in 1947 at the very high price of £222, but soon attracted a reputation for unreliability. Only around 2000 S7s were made before the heavily reworked S8 and S7 De Luxe were introduced in 1949. The S8, with BSA A10 wheels and forks, was about 5mph (8km/h) quicker and 30lb (13.6kg) lighter than its predecessor. Ridden prudently, it proved reliable, but pedestrian. Nonetheless, by December 1952, 10,000 had been built. From then on sales steadily declined, and the range – and the Sunbeam name – was dropped when BSA and Triumph merged in late '56.

63

Triumph

O F LITERALLY hundreds of British motorcycle manufacturers, Triumph is the only one producing motorcycles in any numbers today, and even that in a completely different guise from the original company. Founded in Coventry in 1885 by a German, Siegfried Bettmann, to import and later make bicycles, Triumph built their first motorcycle in 1902. Another German, Bettman's new partner Mauritz Schulte, provided most of the technical input for this, a 1³/₄hp Minerva, and much of their products for the next 20 years. Other machines with proprietary engines (Fafnir, JAP) followed, until the first Triumph engine arrived in 1905. The side-valve 363cc (later up to 500cc) engine was soundly built, earning Triumph motorcycles a reputation for quality and dependability.

Above: The enduring two-stroke 'Baby' Triumph model.
Below: The notorious Model P, a cut-price horror which almost ruined Triumph and certainly made life hard for many of their competitors.

Triumph cycle parts proved similarly robust, notably the famous Triumph sprung fork which was to last into the Twenties. In 1907 Jack Marshall's Triumph placed second in the first TT, winning one year later. By 1910 production was over 3000 machines per year – mainly singles, although a prototype 600cc side-valve twin appeared in 1913. There was also a 225cc two-stroke single, nicknamed the 'Baby' Triumph. During the First World War, no less than 30,000 Triumphs were supplied to the military.

In the Twenties, Triumph introduced two of their most innovative models, the Ricardo and the LS; and one of their worst, the cut-price Model P. 1923 brought the first Triumph four-wheeler, a 1393cc open tourer. Introduced in the same year, the LS was an advanced 350cc side-valve, three-speeder with gear primary drive and an 'automatic' oil pump. Somehow, it failed to inspire the public and was soon withdrawn.

The £43 Model P – the cheapest (and nastiest) 500cc motorcycle ever offered for sale – was Triumph's response to the post-war slump. By the time the improved Mk2 arrived, 3000 employees could produce as many as 1000 Model Ps alone each week at the Priory Street works, and Triumph were vigorously pursuing exports.

The Depression hit Triumph hard, and in 1936 this giant was split up, cars going one way, bikes another – to Ariel's Jack Sangster. As well as rescue, Sangster successively gave two great designers, Val Page and Edward Turner, their big break. Both had cut their teeth at Ariel before moving to Priory Street. Page created a broad new range of singles, as well as Triumph's first four-stroke vertical twin, the 76mph (122km/h) 650cc 6/1 of 1933. Turner later axed the 650, revamped the singles into the stylish Tiger range, and created a twin of his own – the immortal 500cc Speed Twin, first shown in 1937.

After a busy war – Triumph supplied almost 50,000 bikes to the forces, had their factory bombed flat and moved to Meriden – the theme was twins. Not a solitary single featured in the '46 line-up. Telescopic forks appeared, sprung hubs and then swing-arm rear ends, and the 500 twin was boosted to 650cc. The first such model was the T6 Thunderbird of 1949. Just £10 more than the Speed Twin, it soon became Triumph's most desirable model – until a 'hotter' version, the Tiger 110, arrived in '54. There were also off-road twins, notably the TR5 and TR6 Trophy.

A massive boost in sales came after the 1951 creation of an American subsidiary, yet in the same year Triumph was sold to BSA, although the two model ranges would stay separate for many years.

As well as the big stuff, there was the remarkable 199cc T20 Tiger Cub, whose agility and punchy 10bhp engine brought considerable trials success. The Cub was the last truly successful lightweight that Meriden was to make, just as the Bantam was BSA's. In the late Sixties, with Japanese competition growing, the BSA/Triumph locker seemed to contain no convincing response. In desperation a potentially promising new 350 was rushed into production, with catastrophic results. The débâcle caused the BSA Group's overdraft to soar to over £22 million; the bankers pulled the plug and the company collapsed in 1972.

However, the Triumph tale doesn't end there. When a Norton-Villiers rescue plan proposed the closure of Meriden, the workers occupied the factory. The Workers' Cooperative was the result, and it continued to produce Triumph 750cc twins until that in turn succumbed to a lack of new models in 1983. From those ashes arose the miracle of John Bloor's 'new' Triumph, now producing over 15,000 ultra-modern machines per year at the even more space-age Hinckley factory.

Below: The immortal Thunderbird; 650cc of very potent twin. The Americans loved its svelte lines, eager power and agile handling.

TRIUMPH RICARDO

In 1921 the Harry Ricardo-designed Triumph Type R 'Riccy' startled motorcycling. Its cylinder head not only featured a pent-roof combustion chamber, but no less than four valves controlled the gas flow. Bench testing revealed a healthy peak power output of 20bhp at 4600rpm.

In its first TT the underdeveloped machine fared poorly, but a revised version, ridden by Walter

SPECIFICATION	TRIUMPH RICARDO
ENGINE	air-cooled 499cc ohv 4-valve single
POWER	20bhp @ 4600rpm
TRANSMISSION	3-speed
FUEL TANK	N/A
WEIGHT	N/A
TOP SPEED	84mph (135km/h)

Brandish, placed second in 1922. The four-valver had already shown its potential the previous November in taking the world 500cc one-hour record at 76.74mph (123.5km/h), and the British flying mile record at 83.91mph (135.04km/h). In 1922 roadster versions were available for £120.

Regrettably Triumph did not persevere with the Riccy, preferring the Type TT two-valver developed by Victor Horsman. This was to become Triumph's stock competition machine until the early Thirties, also forming the basis of the flagship ST sports model.

Below: Although its competition success was limited, the four valve 'Ricardo' was one of the truly outstanding British machines. Its creator, Harry Ricardo, was one of the pioneering giants of automotive design.

66

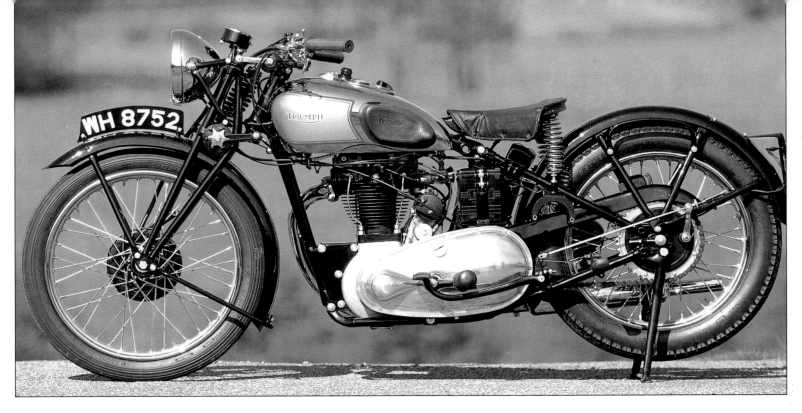

TRIUMPH TIGER 90

One of Edward Turner's first acts on arriving at Priory Street was to re-vamp the capable but staid-looking Triumph singles. The most desirable of the resulting motorcycles was the Tiger 90 – '90' was

SPECIFICATION	TRIUMPH TIGER 90
ENGINE	air-cooled 497cc ohv single
POWER	28bhp @ 5700rpm
TRANSMISSION	4-speed
FUEL TANK	3 gallons (13.6 litres)
WEIGHT (dry)	365lb (166kg)
TOP SPEED	85mph (137km/h)

Above and right: Edward Turner's first major task was to revamp the existing Triumph singles, which he did to great effect with the handsome Tiger 90.

the notional top speed – a development of the previous top-of-the-range 500, the 5/5. The '/5' denoted the most sporting of the available roadster models. All three Tiger singles, the 250cc 70, 350cc 80 and 500cc 90, featured enclosed valvegear, dry sump lubrication, Amal carbs and 6v Lucas Magdyno. The Tiger 90 also boasted a polished con rod and flywheels and hand-finished ports. For an extra £7, a specially equipped competition version was available.

Possibly the most influential motorcycle ever built, Turner's 500cc Speed Twin began four decades of vertical twin domination. These examples date from 1950 (left) and 1953 (below).

TRIUMPH SPEED TWIN

Surely the quintessential British motorcycle, Turner's masterpiece launched Triumph – and Britain – on the road to post-war vertical twins. £77 15s secured a 27bhp four-speed engine in what was essentially a Tiger 90 chassis and running gear but, despite its 'extra' cylinder, the twin weighed little more than the single. Peak power was 27bhp, good for effortless cruising and a top speed approaching 90mph (145km/h). A sports version, the 98mph (158km/h) Tiger 100, soon followed.

SPECIFICATION	TRIUMPH SPEED TWIN
ENGINE	air-cooled 498cc ohv parallel twin
POWER	27bhp @ 6500rpm
TRANSMISSION	4-speed
FUEL TANK	3 gallons (13.6 litres)
WEIGHT (dry)	380lb (172kg)
TOP SPEED	89mph (143km/h)

SPECIFICATION	TRIUMPH T120 BONNEVILLE
ENGINE	air-cooled 649cc ohv parallel twin
POWER	46bhp @ 6500rpm ('R' version: 50bhp)
TRANSMISSION	4-speed (later 5)
FUEL TANK	3 gallons (13.6 litres)
WEIGHT (dry)	399lb (181kg)
TOP SPEED	110mph (177km/h)

Left and below: The zenith of 'Bonnie' development was the 125mph (201km/h) Thruxton model, of which only 58 were built from 1965-66. This was a highly-tuned production racer, boasting many special engine parts, a better chassis and improved brakes. It cost some £365 – £65 more than a 'cooking' Bonneville.

TRIUMPH BONNEVILLE

Named to commemorate Johnny Allen's feat of taking a 650 twin to 214mph (345km/h) at Bonneville Salt Flats in 1956, many regard the early Bonnie as Triumph's best post-war model. Triumph's first twin-carb roadster debuted in 1959, but the initial styling job was curiously staid, with the Speed Twin's nacelled headlamp and distinctly unsporting mudguards. But by 1960, the stylists had got it right. Anyone with £285 to spare could now have this genuine 'ton-plus' machine, perhaps the

fastest standard production motorcycle in the world. Basically, it was a hopped-up Tiger 110, with a tuned light alloy cylinder head.

In 1972 a 51bhp 750cc version, the T140, was added. Scarcely had a five-speeder arrived in 1973 than the Triumph/BSA group went bankrupt. The Meriden Workers Cooperative eventually took over production of the twins, including the limited edition 'Silver Jubilee' T140V. The last Meriden Bonneville was built as the Cooperative collapsed in 1983, although the name will surely re-emerge.

TRIUMPH FURY (BSA BANDIT)

The 349cc twin was an exciting machine – potentially. Designed by two eminently capable men in Bert Hopwood and Doug Hele, it was unveiled to the press and trade in the autumn of 1970. Its parallel twin engine featured twin overhead camshafts, producing 34bhp at 9000rpm, good for over 110mph (177km/h). The engine was a dry sump design, with horizontally-split crankcases and five speeds, and an electric start version would be available. The price was set at £380. Production became a hurried shambles and it never reached the shops.

TRIUMPH TRIDENT 750

In many ways the Triumph Trident, and its sister the BSA Rocket-3, were superior to their Honda CB750 rival. A good one was at least as fast as the Honda. (The first press test Trident, possibly a 'special', clocked almost 130mph/209km/h; others struggled to reach 118mph/190km/h). And the handling, though good, was undoubtedly compromised by the sheer mass of the beast. Nonetheless, it could leave the Honda for dead through the turns.

But the powerplant, imposing as it was, was little more than a stop-gap measure, essentially 1½ Triumph Tigers on a common crankcase. This was the triple that Edward Turner might have designed in 1937, with push-rods rather than overhead camshafts, and crankcases which split vertically, like the twin's. However, housed in a 'Rob North' frame, it became a potent weapon in racing: first, second and third at Daytona in 1971; countless other short-circuit victories; and a unique succession of five production TT wins for the legendary 'Slippery Sam'.

Below: The machine that brought the end: the 350cc dohc BSA Fury. Triumph's Bandit model was essentially identical, and precisely as big a disaster.

SPECIFICATION	TRIUMPH FURY
ENGINE	air-cooled 349cc dohc parallel twin
POWER	34bhp @ 9000rpm
TRANSMISSION	5-speed
FEUL TANK	N/A
WEIGHT	N/A
TOP SPEED	110mph (177km/h)

Left and above: Despite its push-rod engine, the Triumph Trident/BSA Rocket-3 was a hurried but surprisingly able response to the new wave of superbikes coming from Japan. Pictured is a 1974 T150V five-speeder.

SPECIFICATION	TRIUMPH T150 TRIDENT
ENGINE	air-cooled 740cc ohv triple
POWER	58bhp @ 7250rpm
TRANSMISSION	5-speed
FUEL TANK	3 gallons (13.6 litres)
WEIGHT (dry)	503lb (228kg)
TOP SPEED	120mph (193km/h)

Velocite

THE FAMILY firm of Veloce Ltd., despite occasional adventures with twins, scooters and oddball two-strokes, will always be associated with pedigree four-stroke singles. From the outset they were an independent-minded company, often producing designs of great technical novelty. But it is singles for which they are best remembered,

usually in classy gloss black, picked out with gold pin-striping. Indeed, throughout the Sixties they manufactured what became the epitome of British road-going singles: the 350cc Viper and 500cc Venom. And most celebrated of all was the 'Thruxton' Venom, the ultimate street-racing single.

Although a small manufacturer Velocette was

a potent force in racing, claiming eight Junior TT wins between 1926 and '49, and the first 350cc world championships in 1949 and 1950. Indeed, if Velocette had a lasting commercial handicap, it was its sheer addiction to racing.

The company was founded by German-born Johannes Gutgeman (later changed to Goodman), who made the unlikely manufacturing leap from pills to motorcycles. When his first such venture foundered in 1904, he turned to making bicycles, returning to powered two-wheelers in partnership with sons Percy and Eugene in 1910. Most of their early machines were simple two-strokes, but in 1925 Percy designed the Model K, the machine which was to be the blueprint for the company's most prized creations.

In the 1926 Isle of Man Junior TT this overhead cam 350 beat the previously dominant machine – the 'Big Port' AJS – by fully ten minutes. Victory brought considerable sales success, ultimately leading to the first KSS (sports) and KTT (racing) machines of the late Twenties. These were to become the ultimate clubman's race tools for a generation, rivalled only by Norton's Inter and Manx. In the Thirties a less elaborate push-rod single, the MOV, joined the range, later joined by 350 MAC and 500cc MSS models. These, and the GTP 250cc two-stroke, did much to offset the Goodman's expensive obsession with racing, which culminated in the ambitious twin cylinder 'Roarer' –

Left: The cammy KSS was the road-going equivalent of Velocette's full-blown KTT racing machines. This 1939 Mk2 shows the aluminium head adopted in 1938 and has 'benefitted' from a later swing arm conversion.

VELOCETTE KSS

The KSS – Model K 'Super Sports' – arose in the late Twenties out of Velocette's all-conquering TT exploits. A true sister model to the KTT racers, the Mk1 of the early Thirties offered prodigious, free-revving performance for its time. The Mk2 version appeared in 1936, with a much-improved engine, good enough to continue in production well after the Second World War. Regrettably, the bevel-drive cammy engine was prohibitively expensive to produce, causing it to be withdrawn after 1948. From then on, only the pure racing KTT – ultimately the Mk8 – continued to fly Velocette's cammy flag.

Left: Perhaps the most handsome of all the British racing singles, this overhead camshaft KTT Mk8 dates from 1948.

73

yet another British racer killed off by the post-war ban on supercharging.

During the austere years after the Second World War, the emphasis passed to humbler machines, yet often these were designs that reflected Veloce's customary need to be different – notably with the LE 'Noddy Bike'. This led in turn to the air-cooled Valiant and scooterish Vogue, neither of which were any more successful.

But if there was a classic breed of Velo in the post-war years, it was the Viper (350cc) and Venom (500cc) singles. Derived from the MAC and MSS respectively, these evolved by degrees into ever more potent devices, the Clubman's and Thruxton Velos. Along with BSA's Gold Star, they were the ultimate expression of the sporting British single – but by the late Sixties, the market was demanding

even more performance, and a less cantankerous disposition. Yet what finally brought the company down in February 1971 was the development costs of, of all things, the Viceroy scooter. Like much that Veloce produced, the little two-stroke twin with reed valve induction was way ahead of its time. But the factory's classic singles are a far more fitting memorial.

SPECIFICATION	KSS Mk2 (1938)
ENGINE	air-cooled ohc 348cc single
POWER	N/A
TRANSMISSION	4-speed
FUEL TANK	3.5 gallons (16 litres)
WEIGHT (dry)	N/A
TOP SPEED	80mph (129km/h)

Above: On the road, however, post-war sports Velos were all of push-rod design, such as this 500cc Venom model from 1959. The 350cc Viper looked almost identical.

VELOCETTE LE

The LE was a valiant but unsuccessful attempt at producing a machine for civilized commuter motorcycling. It was powered by a near-silent 149cc engine (192cc from 1950) of unusually advanced specifications: liquid-cooled, horizontally-opposed, with a four-bearing crank and alloy heads. A sheet steel 'monocoque' formed the chassis, with integral mudguards and leg-shields. Starting was by pull-handle. It was economical, sedate and sensible – and Veloce could scarcely give them away.

Despite the LE's failure, Veloce plugged on with the same basic engine. First (1956) came the Valiant, a far less radical derivative, with air-cooling and more power (12bhp/66mph/106km/h). The later Vogue harked back to the LE's full coverage, now in fibreglass, and sold even less well than its ancestors.

Velocette's attempts to broaden their market threw up some strange-looking devices, such as the Mk3 LE 'Noddy Bike' (above) and Valiant (left). Both are of a neat and clever design, powered by 192cc horizontally opposed twins, but lacked performance and market appeal. An LE stars regularly in the 'Heartbeat' television series.

SPECIFICATION	VELOCETTE LE
ENGINE	liquid-cooled 149cc side-valve flat twin
POWER	6bhp (192cc version: 8bhp)
TRANSMISSION	3-speed
FUEL TANK	1.25 gallons (5.7 litres)
WEIGHT (dry)	265lb (120kg)
TOP SPEED	50mph (80km/h)

74

VELOCETTE THRUXTON

The 'Thrucky' was the most powerful of all Velocette's roadster singles. Derived from the Clubman, itself a tuned Venom, the model celebrated a similar machine's 1964 victory in the prestigious 500-mile race at Hampshire's Thruxton circuit. From mid-'65 about 1000 'replica' Thruxton's were built at the Hall Green factory.

Powering the Thruxton was a hotted-up version of the standard 499cc Venom overhead-valve engine. Engine modifications included an Amal racing carburettor, high compression pistons (9:1), and special cylinder heads with huge inlet valves, revised porting and hairier cam timing. It was also equipped with close-ratio gears, up-rated forks, clip-on handlebars, rear-set footrests, a humped seat and long-distance fuel tank.

SPECIFICATION	VENOM THRUXTON
ENGINE	air-cooled 499cc ohv single
POWER	up to 41bhp @ 6500rpm
TRANSMISSION	4-speed
FUEL TANK	4.5 gallons (20.5 litres)
WEIGHT (dry)	390lb (177kg)
TOP SPEED	106mph (171km/h) in road trim

Above: As raucous and antisocial as the LE was civilized and dull, the Thruxton Velocette, like Triumph's special Bonneville, took its name from long-distance exploits at the famous Hampshire race circuit.

Although slightly more refined than a Gold Star, it it was a wildly impractical machine. Maintenance, too, was time-consuming. But when it did go, it went well, winning the first 500cc Production TT in 1967, at an average speed of 89.89mph (144.66km/h). A good Thruxton was capable of 120mph (193km/h) in race tune, well up with the fastest twins.

Vincent

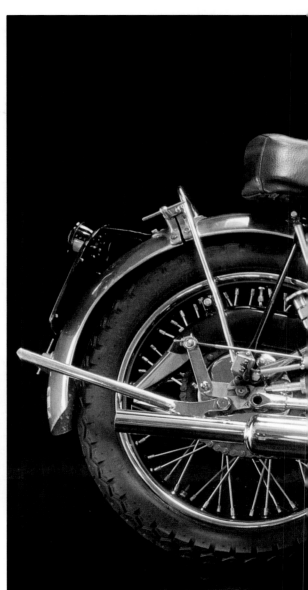

VINCENT IS one of the most gloriously evocative names in British motorcycling, most of all for the creation of a range of V-twins which were for a generation the fastest production machines in the world. The story began with the purchase by Philip Vincent of the HRD company in 1928. HRD, founded by Howard Davies in 1924, had specialized in high-quality sports machines, examples of which had won TTs in 1925 and 1927. The mantle of speed and technical innovation sat easily on Vincent's shoulders.

Early Vincents, like HRD before them, originally used proprietary engines from the likes of Blackburne and JAP. The principal innovation was a novel form of rear suspension of Vincent's own design. After a duff batch of JAP engines was foisted on him at the 1934 TT, Phil Vincent resolved never to be dependent on outside engine suppliers again.

The new breed of engines was largely the work of the ingenious Australian, Phil Irving. First, in 1935, came the Meteor, a high-camshaft 499cc single later capable of 90mph (145km/h) in sports 'Comet' form. Then, in 1936, came the engine for which the Stevenage company was famous: a 998cc V-twin, essentially two Meteor top-ends arranged in a 47 degree Vee on a common crankcase. This became the Series A, dubbed the 'plumber's nightmare' due to an abundance of external oil pipes.

Breathtaking though it was, the Series A had several problems: its 59-inch (1499mm) wheelbase

was ponderously long; and no proprietary transmission could handle its enormous torque.

The result was the post-war Series B Rapide. The transmission was uprated by the use of an ingenious self-servo clutch, and a new gearbox was designed in-unit with the engine. The latter was not only sturdier than its predecessor, but shorter. A radical new 'frame' – basically a box joining the steering head and rear sub-frame, with the engine as a stressed member – allowed Vincent to dispense with front downtubes, further shortening the wheelbase, which now stood at a nimble 56 inches (1422mm). The Rapide was better in every way than the Series A and, with 45bhp and 110mph (177km/h), at least as rapid.

Above and right: The tank badge says it all: not just any old Vincent, but 'The' Vincent. Once the fastest production machine in the world, and for many the first true 'superbike'. This exquisite and original example is a 1951 Rapide.

1948 marked the reappearance of the Vincent singles – the Comet and Meteor – and a sports V-twin, the Black Shadow. Even in 55bhp road trim this monster was capable of 120mph (193km/h). Racing versions, running methanol fuel, produced a staggering 100bhp and went on to claim many racing and record successes. In 1949 the Series C arrived, with Vincent Girdraulic forks in place of Brampton girders (but retaining the Series A's triangulated rear suspension). Produced in touring, sports and racing guises as the Rapide, Black Shadow and Black Lightning respectively, its performance remained unequalled by any production motorcycle until well into the Seventies.

Below: More potent even than the Rapide was the Black Shadow, capable of a genuine 125mph (200km/h) when very few rivals could scrape into three figures.

SPECIFICATION	VINCENT SERIES C BLACK SHADOW
ENGINE	air-cooled 998cc ohv V-twin
HORSEPOWER	55bhp @ 5500rpm
TRANSMISSION	4-speed
FUEL TANK	3.5 gallons (16 litres)
WEIGHT (dry)	455lb (206kg)
TOP SPEED	125mph (201km/h)

Phil Vincent also made an early attempt at market research. The result was the Series D Black Knight and Black Prince, successors to the Rapide and Shadow respectively. Some details, notably coil ignition, were better. But both models were fully enclosed, like giant black scooters. The public was horrified. Series D was quickly reintroduced as 'proper' naked Vincents. But this costly U-turn was the factory's last major act. Sales were tumbling and costs rising, and in 1955 Vincent closed their gates for the last time.

Left: If the idea of a 1000cc scooter appals you now, the Series D had much the same effect when launched in 1954. Below: With a little ingenuity, two of these makes a V-twin. A 1951 500cc Comet single.

In 1955 Russell Wright took a Vincent through the timing lights at Christchurch, New Zealand at 184.83mph (297.45km/h), a new world record.

The trouble was that these hand-crafted machines were prohibitively expensive to produce. Times became particularly hard during the sales slump of 1954, forcing the company to manufacture NSU mopeds and Firefly engines under licence at the Stevenage factory.

SPECIFICATION	VINCENT COMET
ENGINE	air-cooled ohv 499cc single
HORSEPOWER	28bhp @ 5800rpm
TRANSMISSION	4-speed
FUEL TANK	3.75 gallons (17 litres)
WEIGHT (dry)	400lb (181kg)
TOP SPEED	88mph (142km/h)

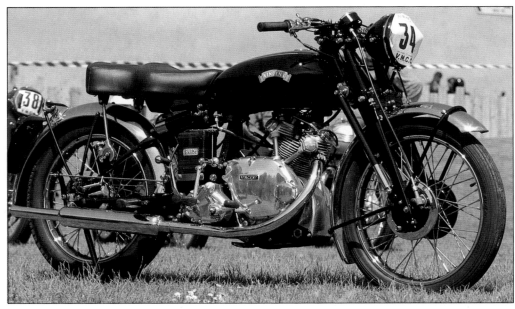

Index